THE ART PROJECT

EMILYA COLLIVER

Also by Emilya Colliver
*Making Art Matter: How to work with
artists to bring art into our buildings,
spaces and communities*

With over 20 years of experience in the art world across public and
private art, Emilya is passionate about supporting Australian art and
the practitioners who create it. Her work is characterised by strong
leadership, inclusivity, deep stakeholder engagement and a focus
on creating outcomes.

Emilya's passion is supporting Australian art and creative practitioners.
Before launching Art Pharmacy, she studied Art History at SOAS and
UCL in London. She also worked for top art institutions and galleries –
Lisson Gallery, Hauser & Wirth, The British Museum and Eskenazi – as well
as managing the collection of James Birch Esq. (fun art collector and
a mentor to Emilya).

Emilya was the first Director of The Other Art Fair in (Australia) in 2015.
She has spoken at Global Cities After Dark conference (2017), acted as
a long-term MCA Young Ambassadors Committee member (2013–2020)
and co-founded the Place Academy collaboration (2018); she was
appointed to the City of Sydney's Nightlife and Creative Sector Advisory
Panel (2018) as well as the Randwick City Council Night-Time Economy
Advisory Committee (2018). She has been a member of EO Sydney (2019),
and now sits as a Benefaction Committee Member for the Biennale
of Sydney (2019) and was City of Sydney Art & About Judge 2021.

She is also involved in non-fungible tokens (NFTs) and Blockchain,
and is currently building her own platform to support Australian
and international artists.

THE ART PROJECT
EMILYA COLLIVER

A HANDBOOK
FOR THE PUBLIC AND
PRIVATE SECTORS

We acknowledge the Traditional Custodians of the land where we live and work, and pay our respects to the Gadigal people of the Eora nation on which our office stands. We recognise the First Nations peoples as the original artists and part of the world's oldest living culture.

First published in 2023 by Emilya Colliver

A catalogue entry is for this work is available
from the National Library of Australia.

ISBN: 978-1-922764-7-68

artpharmacy.com.au
iloveart@artpharmacy.com.au
@artpharmacy

Disclaimer
The material in this publication is of the nature of general comment only, and does not represent professional advice. It is not intended to provide specific guidance for particular circumstances and it should not be relied on as the basis for any decision to take action or not take action on any matter which it covers. Readers should obtain professional advice where appropriate, before making any such decision. To the maximum extent permitted by law, the author and publisher disclaim all responsibility and liability to any person, arising directly or indirectly from any person taking or not taking action based on the information in this publication.

Cover, interior and illustrations by Thought & Found
Printed by Ingram Spark

This book is dedicated to my husband, Giles,
and our two vibrant and spirited children,
Scarlett and Hugo.

To my grandmother,
Oma, who I still miss so much.

And to all the artists and creatives I have worked
with over the years, for always inspiring me.

CONTENTS

FOREWORD

Australia is well ahead of many western countries in its community arts engagement projects. Sadly, the same cannot be said of many of its corporate art collections and displays. Some of our best civic architecture is let down by safe, uninspiring artworks chosen to hang back, soaking up the shadows while the rest of the world steps forward with style and confidence.

Art Pharmacy's founding curator Emilya Colliver's inspiring how-to guide provides a path to the possibilities great art can provide. The results of her research and engagement with some of our country's largest, most successful companies should be proof enough to anyone left doubting the value of engaging with art in our society.

Colliver's invitation for corporations to seize the opportunity to play a leading role in supporting our vibrant arts community could not come at a better time. Her rallying cry is heartfelt and highly informed. From the moment you step aboard Art Pharmacy's learning curve with *The Art Project,* from your first open-hearted encounter with the new art forms Colliver presents, the world around you will never look quite the same again. – Jane Rankin-Reid

INTRODUCTION

Are you a project manager, marketing manager or architect who has an interest in delivering a successful art project for your organisation? Are you overseeing the development of an art strategy or putting together a corporate art collection? If so, then this book is for you.

My intention in writing *The Art Project* is to make you feel comfortable with the process of developing and managing an art project, and to empower you to work successfully with creative practitioners and artists – that is, to help you implement art within projects and give you art confidence within your organisation.

I'll cover what you'll need to consider when you commission an artwork for a project. We'll look at the various dos and don'ts of each step of the process, from establishing a strong art narrative to the installation of the final artwork. I'll also talk you through how to create a corporate art collection as an alternative to commissioning new work.

My name is Emilya Colliver. I run Art Pharmacy, a successful creative arts consultancy business based in Sydney, Australia. Together with my team, I work with councils, government bodies and developers, as well as corporate and private clients interested in art and the impact it can have on a space. This book is based on my own extensive experience in the art world – 20 years of it, with ten of those years as an independent consultant and creative practitioner.

While we work with many different clients, the focus of this book is to assist those who would like to commission artists to work on developments, or those who would like to work with artists in a corporate setting. This is Art Pharmacy's niche and what we do best.

In this book, I'll give you practical and specific advice based on my own learnings in the art industry, and share the quick solutions and problem-solving tactics I've honed on numerous projects that will help you resolve the issues you may encounter. So, if you're looking to do the right thing with your art project but are unsure how or where to start, I'm here to help.

While there is no arts degree out there on how to be an art consultant, my background includes a degree in History and Archaeology from London (UCL and SOAS University) that has been a great foundation for what I do. Yet it is my real-life experience that has formed and built my knowledge in this area. It's easy to call yourself an art consultant – you don't really need any qualifications – but it's experience that makes the difference. That is why I have written this book.

I never thought I would be a writer. In all honesty, writing isn't easy. But deep down, I knew that I needed to share with others what I have learnt. I see myself as an educator in this space and it is important to me that there is a standard of practice that everyone can work towards in this business. My aim is for this book to become that standard. I'd like to see this book included in TAFE, university and art school syllabuses; to be used when considering policy development; and to be consulted by national property councils when looking at planning new developments.

When I started Art Pharmacy ten years ago, with my nine-month-old daughter in tow, launching my own independent art consultancy was a sink or swim scenario. There was virtually no information out there to help me. Even now, there is a shortage of published material that comprehensively covers the complexities of commissioning art in the public realm, the development of placemaking ideas and the various ways of writing an art strategy. This book and my previous work, *Making Art Matter*, are the first steps in my plan to share knowledge with those who want to implement art in corporate and public spaces.

My long-term goal is to start a wellbeing centre in rural Australia where senior management, entrepreneurs and those with small businesses can come together to reflect on business goals and write impactful models that incorporate art into developments and public spaces, all while surrounded by the beauty of our land. It is very important for business owners, managers and their staff to take time out to recharge and reflect on the projects that really mean something to them and their organisation. My wellbeing space will be designed to provide opportunities to learn about cultural, art and placemaking theories, and to inspire all who visit it because I strongly believe supporting staff and client wellbeing is the future. My idea is still in its early stages but is continually blossoming with fresh buds of possibility.

For now, I'd like to create a catalyst for change in the small and tightly guarded art world. The arts have been decimated in recent years due to COVID-19, but if history has anything to tell us, they will rise again. Perhaps this will be our renaissance. But to make this happen, art needs to be present, accessible and visible. Just as public parks have become mandated in new building developments, so has art. It took a while to achieve, but the inclusion of public art in these projects is no longer seen as simply a box to tick.

This new outlook has encouraged and fostered viable careers in the arts. We can now encourage our children to work as artists or creatives because there are new and exciting career paths open to them.

The social and economic benefits of public art are well researched. There's no doubt that art in a public space can engage communities and neighbourhoods, and draw visitors from far and wide. Presenting work in a public space also offers artists the opportunity to make important and impactful commentary to general audiences outside an institutional context.

Being an art consultant in this space is a delicate balance between push and pull. I'd like to thank all the artists, creatives and clients I have worked with in my ten years of art consultancy, and in the 20 years I've worked in the art world – we are all teachers in life, and you have all helped me grow and learn along the way. I am truly grateful to all of you who have helped Art Pharmacy achieve the success it has had over the past decade, especially through a global pandemic.

One thing I know is that we never stop learning. The joy and power of art is waiting for you to discover it. So, go forward and be bold. Be authentic, be curious and be brave. – Emilya Colliver

DELIVERING A SUCCESSFUL PROJECT

ART

THE   01
ART PROJECT

Delivering a successful art project involves many steps – it is a creative journey.

WHAT IS AN ART PROJECT?

An art project is a project dedicated to the commissioning and creation of an artwork that is site-specific and community-centric.

This book is intended as a guide for corporations, developers, government bodies and councils that are seeking to incorporate art into new or refurbished developments – essentially those who want artwork to fill a specific space and engage a specific audience.

As we know, art comes in all shapes and sizes, as well as in a variety of mediums. Pieces of art can span different projects and timelines. An art project could involve the creation of anything from a painted mural to a large-scale sculpture or an activation. All art projects are informed by an art strategy, and involve working with artists and stakeholders to deliver the right artwork within a particular timeframe.

However, a successful art project is much more than commissioning (or buying) a piece of art – it involves developing a narrative that will inspire an artist to create an artwork that will communicate your message to the local community. Delivering a successful art project involves many steps – it is a creative journey.

COMMISSION VERSUS PURCHASE PROCESS

There are two ways to secure the right artwork for a space: through commission or purchase. Purchasing an artwork involves buying a pre-existing work that is the right fit for the space or project. Commissioning involves creating an art strategy and sourcing an artist who can then create the artwork you're looking for. The commission will express the vision of the project, and you will work with that artist to create an artwork within the budget, dimensions and materials that are best suited for the project.

> With a commissioned work, the artist designs the piece specifically for you, rather than creating a piece that they then sell to the right buyer.

There is a common misconception that artists will have the perfect piece of art waiting to find a home, but this is often not the case. Purchasing an artwork means you have no say over the final work, as it already exists, so you might be compromising certain requirements if the piece doesn't meet them. Commissioning the work allows for greater control over the design and outcome, but often involves more resources from the artist and buyer.

THE PERKS OF COMMISSIONING A BESPOKE ARTWORK

Art Pharmacy has often been called in at the last minute to solve an art issue, such as a refurbishment or lobby fit-out requiring a hero piece. For example, a client wants something to make a colourful impact for a corporate or government tenant; an artwork large enough to hang comfortably on a wall four metres long. They go to a gallerist but the content, artistic style and size of artwork they want is not available. That's when they'll come to us and ask us to manage the process of finding the perfect artwork for their foyer.

People can have the expectation that artists will have that perfect artwork in their studio waiting to find a home, but this isn't necessarily the case. It is generally unlikely that artists will have an artwork at the right size – especially a huge painting – available at any given time. Therefore, in the example above, the client would have been better off commissioning a work specifically for the space rather than trying to retrofit an existing artwork to their needs.

To me, it really makes sense for organisations to commission a bespoke artwork for their project, especially if it is a new development. This is not unlike having custom-designed furniture made for a specific space. If you commission an artwork, you can indicate in your artist brief the size, colours and intent of the artwork you would like to have.

Here are a few more reasons why I recommend commissioning bespoke artwork for your art project.

Timing

Once an artist has painted an artwork, they want it out of their studio as soon as possible to make room for the next project. Unless you time your purchase correctly, you may miss out. If you commission an artwork, you won't lose out on the artwork you want as it is being made especially for you.

Size

If you are looking for a large artwork, you may be out of luck. Art studios in metropolitan areas tend to be small and can't hold large, or many, works of art, so you may not find the size you want. Commissioning a work ensures you get the right size as well as a piece that is made with your site in mind.

Quality

While galleries do hold artwork from a variety of artists, both on show and in storage, the size and subject matter of these pieces may not suit your space. Often the artworks kept in storage are those that have not sold at exhibition. While these may still be good, if you commission an artwork, you will be assured of the quality of the final piece and that it will answer your project's aims the way you would like it to.

Thematic Relevance

Artists are inspired by what they see around them and what is important to them – an artwork is an expression of an artist's soul. When they create an artwork, they may focus on specific ideas – such as climate or political issues – or have a specific style. While some artists may have two sides to their practice, one covering commercial work and one that consists of work based on their own personal reflections, their themes may not be relevant to your organisation's project or align with its values.

If you choose to commission an artist, you can employ one you are drawn to, one whose work might already relate to your own art project's narrative. You can research their previous work and how they have been received by the public. Doing this will enable you to find an artist who aligns with your organisation's values and mission.

Remember that although commissioning an artist will give you a better idea of what to expect from the artwork, the brief you give to the artist shouldn't be too rigid. You need to give the artist parameters and be clear on what you want, but you don't want to tell them exactly what to do. You are employing them to express their artistic response to your art narrative.

Apart from being able to cater to specific art needs, what I love about commissioning an artwork is that the artist is paid to make original artwork in their studio in their own time. In contrast to this, an artist exhibiting in a gallery has no guarantee that they will sell their artworks. They also lose out financially through the sale percentage the gallery takes. By commissioning a bespoke artwork for your space, you are supporting a local artist in the best way possible and, by extension, supporting the broader creative community.

Another point on working with galleries is that often the commission structures can get a little complicated, and the gallery may not have much experience in working in the public art realm or with corporate clients. Unless you are working directly with one gallery only on your art project, you will likely have better success in finding what you want with the help of an art consultant.

If you do not wish to commission an artwork and prefer to buy from a gallery, then having an art consultant on board will help you source artwork from multiple galleries. They can produce a longlist of artists, help you whittle it down to a shortlist and then assist you with selecting the final piece/s. If you go this way, remember to give your consultant enough time to ensure this process is done carefully and correctly.

Similarly, if you want to go down the commission route and don't feel confident in doing it on your own, an art consultant can help you and your art project manager do this. There are still a number of important steps to follow to ensure the success of your art project. I will outline these in detail in the coming chapters.

GOLDEN POINTS

01 Commissioning an artwork will give you something original that will be created specifically for your site and the community that uses the space.

02 By supporting the artist to create something new for you, you support their practice and the wider creative community.

03 When commissioning work, select an artist you are drawn to and who speaks to your organisation's values and mission.

GREAT POWER OF ART IS IN ITS EXTRAVAGANCE THE

THE DIFFERENT TYPES OF ART PROJECTS

Public art can be controversial, political and thought-provoking, or bring about unity through memorial or community representation.

PUBLIC ART

The breadth of possibilities with public art is limitless. It can elevate a space through aesthetic gain, or it can make a statement. Public art can express community values and culture, enhance or contrast the natural environment, reflect common opinions or question public assumptions. Public art can be controversial, political and thought-provoking, or bring about unity through memorial or community representation.

THE CORPORATE ART COLLECTION

Not everyone who wants art in their space or workplace will want to commission an artwork. Commissioning a creative project can be exciting but it might be too time-consuming or costly for you. An alternative is an acquisitive model where you select and purchase art to create a corporate collection. You will still, however, need to consider every acquisition carefully; a collection of art that depicts subject matter no one can relate to has the potential to work against you. It's for this reason that I recommend you consider having your art collection curated.

Why Start an Art Collection?

Art Pharmacy has frequently been asked to curate collections for corporate clients. Generally, this includes assisting the company to create or choose a narrative, selecting artists for the company's approval, procuring the art, and framing and installing the artworks.

For us, this is about shaping the future of workplaces. Art can communicate stories, engage staff and amplify key points of difference. All of these can deliver distinct and dynamic outcomes for businesses – including activating the space; connecting staff to the building, the business and each other; and creating a distinctive environment everyone can be proud of.

If you are a business owner or CEO, an art collection can resonate both with your workforce and your clients. For this to happen effectively, it should reflect your company's work culture and ethics. A great art collection that is accessible to everyone in your organisation is also a fantastic way to retain staff – having art hanging on your walls improves morale and keeps people happy.

Your collection can be tailored to reflect the dynamism of your company. There is nothing less inspiring to a client than meeting you in an office that has bland, unimaginative art hanging on the wall, or worse – no art at all.

So, consider the following as good reasons for creating a collection:
- increased employee and visitor engagement
- the potential for a visual expression of your corporate responsibility
- a way to express the brand story of your business
- an opportunity to give back to your community and support a creative industry in a sustainable way
- creating a fun, interesting and dynamic office you can proudly show off to your clients.

How to Begin

If you want to be a cook, you buy cookbooks and utensils then develop your skills. Collecting art is similar – you need to build your skills and refine your taste. You don't need to buy the first thing that you see! It takes time to get a sense of what will suit your organisation. You can make a start by following the progress of some artists whose work you like. With so much exciting talent in Australia, it's never been easier to build a strong art collection and support local artists at the same time.

Keep in mind that every great collection starts with purchasing a single piece of art. As you learn about what you like and what suits your organisation, note down some clear guidelines for the collection (the narrative of the collection). If you don't feel confident doing this on your own, an art consultant or curator can help you do this.

Questions to think about as you begin the process of collecting:
- What medium do you really find compelling? For example, do you love video art, sculpture or painting?
- When you find an artwork you like, consider how it will fit in the space you intend it to go. How will it look in relation to its surroundings?
- Look at the size of the piece. Do you have enough wall space for it?
- If you like video art, will a digital screen be something that will fit in the space? Will it need to be installed in a particular way?
- Think about what the artwork communicates. What impact do you want the artwork to have on your clients and on your staff? Does the artwork achieve that?

The way you shape your collection will depend on what you want your organisation to communicate to your staff, clients and the public.

You may consider focusing on the medium, selecting mainly digital artworks or photographs; or an art style, such as landscape or abstract artworks; or on an art movement, such as modernism, post-structuralism or surrealism. You might want to support a particular section of the creative community, such as artists from culturally diverse backgrounds, First Nations artists or female artists.

Alternatively, you might want to create your own art narrative – perhaps something fun and accessible. This can be approachable and can help your staff connect with the collection. A narrative that is relatable can guide you when choosing new artworks for the collection that will resonate with your staff.

Whichever way you go, ensure your narrative can function as a broad linking element for the pieces in your collection. Remember to stick to your theme when choosing pieces; doing so will support the integrity of the collection. As you build the collection, try to outline a few clear directions that can be used together with your art narrative when purchasing a work. This way, if there is someone within your company interested in bringing in a new artwork or introducing a new artist (and remember, it's always good to support a potential creative pioneer), you can refer to the art narrative guideline to see if the artist and their work fit into the collection. Every artist invests something of themselves in their work and it's well worth discovering the story behind the piece you're thinking of having in the collection, so do your research on them as well. That way you will know if their story fits with yours.

If you have an art committee (and it's useful to have one for curating a collection) make sure they are across the art narrative and are available to meet when selecting new artworks to add to the collection. If you are planning on adding artworks regularly, consider having quarterly meetings with your committee where new works can be discussed.

If you think you won't have time to manage the collection yourself, find someone in your organisation with an affinity for art to manage the art collection for you, or use an art consultant.

Another way to add to your collection and support the creative community is for your company to start an art prize. Many firms do this now, and they do it with purpose and intent. Macquarie Bank, for example, has done a fabulous job of hosting yearly art prizes. If you are interested in this idea, I strongly suggest you hire an art consultant or art contractor experienced in running art prizes as they can set everything up for you and manage the event and its outcome. They are specialists in this area and will ensure everything is done the right way.

Focusing on your art narrative when purchasing works helps to build a meaningful art collection. You'll be able to tell this story to visitors or clients who come to your office and use it to explain how the art collection was formed.

Sharing the story of your collection is also a wonderful way to engage staff. They will develop a better understanding of the collection and will feel more confident in passing this on to others. You can also involve them in the selection of a new piece by asking them to vote on potential new additions.

We encourage you to use the artworks on company documents such as annual reports, as long as you have permission from the artists to do so. This is a great way of increasing the visibility of the artworks for both your staff and clients.

Knowledge is Power

The more you know about art, the easier it will be for you to make informed choices for your collection. It is worthwhile to research artists you like and how they create their artworks. An art curator or art consultant can help you with this, but there are also many books to read about artists, art collections and collecting that will provide you with valuable information. Consider visiting your local art galleries and sign up to their newsletters to find out what exhibitions are coming and when. Take the time to explore the art world; learn about artists you like, find out where they studied and discover if their style is established or still developing. Be curious when learning.

Think about creating a wide-ranging collection by including works by all kinds of artists – emerging, mid-tier and established. Selecting works by emerging artists in particular can provide you with great pieces at an affordable price. And you never know – the artist might become a big name in the future, which will increase the value of your collection.

Budget

Before you start spending, I suggest you devise a budget that clearly identifies how much you can afford and then allocate this for acquiring the pieces. Always get approval on this budget from your Chief Financial Officer. If you intend to build a collection incrementally, you might think about putting aside an amount every year just for purchasing art. If you decide to set up an art committee or advisory board, they can give you advice on acquisitions and keep you on track with the budget.

When you have your budget, start to explore what is available on the market. Remember to keep your art narrative in mind when purchasing a new work so that you don't waste your budget on works that won't fit with the rest of the collection. Also, always be clear about your budget with the gallery or art consultant you work with. If you are unsure about the buying capacity of your budget, ask them if it is sufficient for what you are trying to achieve. For example, a small budget of a few thousand dollars will not be adequate to build a collection that will be in a multimillion-dollar building, but it may work for a small suite of offices. Talk to your gallery or consultant – they can help you review your budget if necessary.

On the other hand, if money is no object, you may consider buying an existing collection to get your new one started. This is an option if the collection you want to buy fits with your narrative. Or you may consider building your narrative around the existing collection's story.

DIGITAL ART

Digital art in the public realm has an established history dating back to the 1960s. It has exploded onto the scene in the last few years with the rise of the screens that we see all over our cities and public places – including transport hubs, train stations, shopping centres, sports stadiums, domestic and international airports, and in the foyers of commercial buildings.

Art Pharmacy has encountered interest from our commercial and public art clients who are intrigued and have the desire to procure digital and immersive art. We have been managing this for years and have a good understanding of the perks and pitfalls. One of the biggest perks is that you can easily change the digital art on display at the click of a button as long as the content management system (CMS) is up to date. Suddenly, a world of art is literally at your fingertips!

The ease of implementing digital art is one of the reasons that it is an incredible way to engage the community. The appeal of digital art reaches beyond an initial captivation by its aesthetic; it is a whole new way for people to engage with art in a manner that is far more accessible. It is no wonder our clients see it as a solution to increasing employee satisfaction, attracting clients and visitors, and strategic public placemaking. Digital art, like our digital world, is connecting us more than ever.

   THE DIFFERENT TYPES OF ART PROJECTS

A concern can arise that digital art will clash or compete with advertising. We have seen digital art used to advertise, or for community messaging, such as about COVID-19; however, as art consultants, we really see this as an opportunity to engage the community through art that can enhance our environment. A time to pause and reflect in our busy lives.

It is important to think in advance about the content you will have on your screen and consider the location of the screen, and the local demographic. I have seen huge TVs that have been installed, with a cost upward of thousands to millions of dollars, that have been left blank or switched off because no budget was allocated for digital artwork as an operation expense. It is really important that if you're managing a screen, you are also thinking about the content long term. This needs to be planned in advance!

Sugar Glider Digital

At Art Pharmacy, we have embraced this trend in digital art by starting our own digital-art-based project called 'Sugar Glider Digital'. We have been curating digital and immersive artworks in the public realm and delivering cultural placemaking strategies. The idea was birthed after we successfully managed seven digital art projects over the last few years. Due to this growing demand, the appeal of the art form and the ability to turn around the digital work quickly for our clients, we decided to give this area more space to grow. There are countless opportunities for the inclusion of digital artwork in corporate, public and development settings. This platform allows our clients to work with a subscription as well as the option to purchase or commission curated digital art, and gives our more traditional artists the chance to enter the digital sphere to capture new audiences.

Think about it: how many blank, unengaging television screens do you see in lobby spaces? Too many! This is just one of the reasons we decided to offer more digital art to our clients.

There are three ways to think about digital art content for your screens:

01 Subscription model – artwork that is delivered on a rotating basis and works within the marketing calendar. For example, artworks that relate to the Spring Racing Carnival, Lunar New Year celebrations, Christmas or Easter.

02 Managing the commissioning of a digital artwork where you select a digital artist and then over 8–12 weeks an artwork is created.

03 Licensing an existing digital artwork for a period of time that is pre-agreed with a contract.

Note, as all screens are different sizes, angles and resolutions and most of the time the digital artwork will need to be formatted or calibrated for the screen, this will require technical assistance to meet the resolution. The above three options range from a few weeks to a few months.

Digital Art and NFTs

Generally, digital art fits into an ever-evolving list of categories: classical, hybrid, environmental, 3D-art, generative, illustrative, code, digital collage or even generated art that uses algorithmic codes to create an output, in a sort of unique 'machine and artist' type collaboration. Programming these codes requires skill and intentionality.

Digital art is also closely linked to the rise of Web3, the next generation of the internet built on new technologies such as blockchain, cryptocurrency and non-fungible tokens (NFTs). Artists have been quick to experiment with these new technologies – it's like having a new canvas or medium to work with. For example, you can mint your artworks into multiple digital editions called NFTs, fractionalise a larger work into collectible NFT components, incorporate an interactive token-currency into artworks through embedding QR codes, or exhibit in a metaverse gallery. The possibilities are endless, and it makes sense that artists, society's creative pioneers, are at the helm of this new wave!

NFTs allow for a wealth of new opportunities for distributing art and protecting artists' copyright. The creator of an art NFT, through the process of 'minting' the NFT, gives their work a stamp of authenticity and ownership, verified using blockchain. Due to the technology used, each NFT is non-fungible (as the name states). This means that each NFT is unique and not interchangeable with any other NFT. It is a one-of-a-kind asset. This also benefits buyers and collectors, who can verify the provenance of NFT art, and be assured of its value.

 THE DIFFERENT TYPES OF ART PROJECTS

Environmental Concerns

Despite the potential to reform the art world, digital art is also facing considerable criticism due to its high environmental impact. A recent study by the Cambridge Bitcoin Electricity Consumption Index found that the amount of electricity that mining Bitcoin consumes in one year is equal to that used to power Malaysia, Sweden or Ukraine.[1] For artists, there comes a huge carbon footprint from the processes of minting, bidding on, cancelling, selling and transferring ownership of NFTs.

There are efforts being made to shift the energy consumption of the blockchain. For example, in 2021, artist Damien Hurst launched a collection of NFTs on the new Palm sidechain, which is 99% more energy efficient than other currencies such as Ethereum and Bitcoin.[2] Other artists are also passionate about making NFTs more sustainable and pushing for carbon offsets and carbon-negative platforms on which to sell their art. Carbon-neutral currencies are increasingly gaining traction and credibility, and are fast becoming the preferred place for artists to sell their works.

One of the reasons Art Pharmacy have gone digital is to reduce our carbon footprint.

Traditional art creates large amounts of waste. Think about the resources required to create, transport, install and de-install artworks. A single work could travel thousands of kilometres by plane, truck, and car, wrapped in layers of plastic and paper. A digital artwork is a single file, that requires the click of a button to display anywhere.

However, we know there is still a long way to go, and we are on the research and development journey to make digital art part of the solution. We only use screens and digital displays that are low-wattage LED, and as much as possible run on alternate sources of energy.

1   Bitcoin's Energy Consumption Is A Highly Charged Debate – Who's Right?, 2021, www.forbes.com/sites/lawrencewinter meyer/2021/03/10/bitcoins-energy-consumption-is-a-highly-charged-debate--whos-right/?sh=14099c7e7e78
2   NFT breakthrough, 2021, www.theartnewspaper.com/2021/03/30/nft-breakthrough-ethereum-co-founder-joe-lubin-creates-99percent-energy-efficient-blockchainand-damien-hirst-is-its-first-artist

GOLDEN POINTS

01 Digital art is on the rise. There is a trend towards the digital among art collectors and corporate clients. It is a great way to increase audience engagement through new media and can be changed with the flick of a button.

02 Digital art is easy to replace once the screens have been installed. Make sure you have an easy-to-use CMS.

03 Think about your digital content before you have even installed your screen, and make plans accordingly. Remember to plan for a yearly budget as this is an ongoing operating expense.

04 Content can engage the community, in the office, a shopping centre or an airport. Think of the artwork as an opportunity to pause and reflect.

05 Digital art can reduce your ecological footprint.

06 Artists are embracing NFTs as a new way to create, share and protect their art.

ACTIVATIONS

Art activations are creative installations that engage the public and draw attention to a bigger idea – ranging from product launches, to celebrating a significant day in the calendar or honouring cultural events.

Businesses, councils and public entities use the power of the arts to activate campaigns, elevate celebrations and promote experiences that would otherwise garner minimal attention. They serve as a critical element in growing the vitality and culture of our communities, by creating vibrant, engaging spaces that would otherwise be idle, modest or bare. Art creates intrigue and can act as placemaking provocateurs in campaigns that desire conversation or dispute. Even a modest investment in art activations can generate significant return for businesses through higher engagement and viewer participation.

Art's great power is in its extravagance and playfulness. For significant moments in time, campaigns and celebrations, traditional forms of advertising are often not enough to get wider engagement; whereas art is a less obvious and sought-out marketing tactic, which often procures bigger results due to its unexpected nature. The underlying value of art is that it invites audience participation by drawing attention to the unordinary, which is why art activations are so valuable.

Art's great power
is in its extravagance
and playfulness.

Studio Visits

If you are interested in the work of a local artist, consider organising a meeting with them at their studio. Discuss the possibility with your art consultant as they'll be able to find out if the artist is open to the idea, and can set up a meeting for you. Going to the artist's studio is a great way to see their work in the flesh and to get to know the artist. If you meet an artist you like but they don't have a suitable work available, you may decide to commission a work from them. If you choose to do this, then simply follow the procedure for commissioning an artwork outlined in this book.

Photographs and Prints

When considering including photographs and/or prints in your collection, make sure you find out how and where on the piece the artist will sign and number the edition. All photographers and printmakers should do this, but it is always worth checking and documenting.

Framing

If you expect the artwork to be framed before delivery, make sure that this is part of your purchase agreement with the artist. Discuss what kind of frame they will use and whether the artwork will be ready for hanging. If the artist isn't organising the framing, they will be able to give you a list of framers that are trustworthy, or your art consultant can assist you.

In general, artworks should be ready to hang and should include D-rings. If your organisation is a hotel, then security screws are a must.

If you are commissioning a range of artworks from different artists, they will probably each use their own framer. If this is the case, the collection could look a little disjointed. If this is of concern to you, I recommend you organise the framing yourself so that you can have one framer do all the works in a consistent way. By doing this, each frame will be of the same quality and you can achieve a more cohesive look for your art collection.

Art Couriers

We always recommend using a specialist art courier for delivering your work as they will have insurance that, for the period of pickup, transport and delivery, will cover the artwork. Get the courier's details, including booking and tracking numbers, as well as a mobile number for the driver, and provide them with your contact number.

Note that the courier is responsible for any damage to the artwork during delivery and must replace your item if serious damage occurs. Ask the artist to provide photos of the work prior to dispatch so you can check the work for damage when it arrives.

Installing Artworks

You will need a specialist installer to install each work in your collection; someone who is knowledgeable at taking care of artworks and installing them correctly. They will need their own insurance and should provide you with references, which you must check. Alternatively, you could go through your art consultant or your gallery to find a specialist installer. Always use a professional for this work and make sure they bring all their own equipment (including a spirit level) and that they use white gloves when handling the pieces. This is essential to protect the artwork; it will minimise the risk of damage and/or leaving fingerprints on works made from or framed behind glass.

If you need to have a hanging system installed, make sure you have someone who knows what they are doing and clearly indicate where the hanging rails should go – you don't want to find them somewhere unexpected.

It's also a good idea to be at the site when the artwork is being installed so that you can confirm each piece is being placed correctly.

There are specific rules and styles for hanging art, from centring each artwork in the collection to creating what's known as 'salon-style' layout, through to hanging the works in a specific way around furniture or to average eye height. Every scenario is different, but the most important thing is that you should love the way your art is displayed.

Plaques

Each artwork should have a plaque that provides details of the work. Try not to make them too lengthy – it is better to be concise and to the point. I also recommend using a material that is suitable for both indoor and outdoor locations. Please find an example of a plaque in the chapter – The Creation of a Legacy – The Lifetime of the Artwork.

Maintenance Report

Every artwork in your collection should have a maintenance report provided to you by the artist. This should be kept with all the other documentation you have collected about the artwork, including the art narrative, a short biography of the artist and a picture of the artwork, and be readily available for anyone who may need to refer to it.

Following are a few examples of maintenance reports.

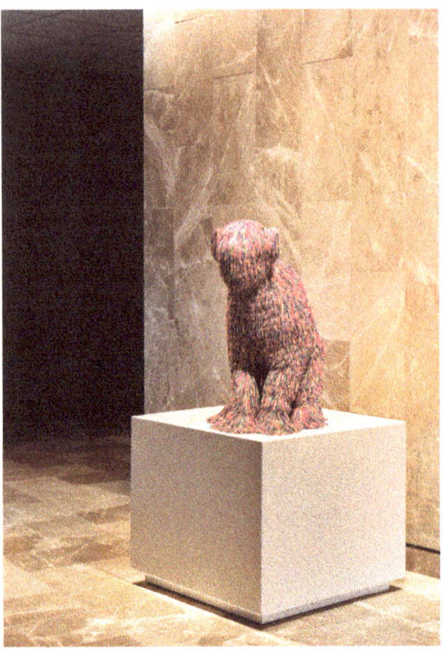

Artist: Troy Emery
Instagram: @troyemery
Location: Melbourne-based artist

Title: Late Night Rainbow, 2020

Materials: Polyester, polyurethane, pins, adhesive

01

Maintenance Report – Example 1

About the Artist: Troy Emery is an artist based in Melbourne and has an art practice encompassing sculpture, painting, and drawing. He works primarily with textiles in a sculptural practice to produce animal-like forms. His artwork examines the discourse surrounding the delineation between fine arts and craft, as well as animals as both entrenched decorative motifs and tokens of ecological ruination.

Maintenance: Do not touch sculptures unless handling is necessary. Textiles easily pick up soil and oils. The body gives off acids and oils through its pores that can damage textiles. If you must move the work, remove any jewellery that could snag or catch on the textiles. We recommend wearing cotton gloves when removing dust, which should be done by gently brushing the dust away from the artwork.

THE DIFFERENT TYPES OF ART PROJECTS

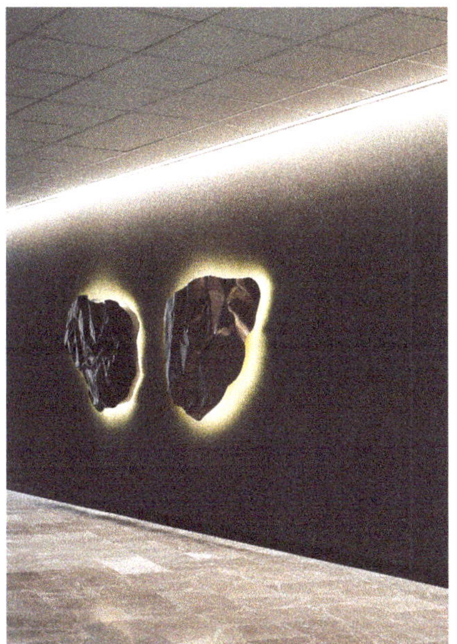

Artist: Jonathan Ben-Tovim
Instagram: @btd___
Location: Melbourne-based artist

Title: Crash Diptych, 2020

Materials: Beaten car bonnet
panels, automotive spray paint,
steel, LED light source

02 Maintenance Report – Example 2

About the Work: Crash Diptych explores the idea of taking something discarded or damaged and turning it into something of surprising beauty. The artwork's outer surfaces are made from upcycled car bonnets sourced from the wrecker yards of the outer northern industrial suburbs of Melbourne. The panels are carefully contorted, and a silhouette is cut out that relates to the bumps and curves. The panels are then sandblasted and given an automotive paint spray to express the rippling surface.

Maintenance: The front crumpled surfaces should be regularly dusted with a soft fibre dusting brush. If further cleaning is required, a damp cloth can be used to gently wipe the front surface. Do not spray the fixture with water or get the rear lighting elements wet when cleaning.

Handling: The fixture uses low voltage LEDs connected to a mains outlet behind the front surface. If the artwork needs to be removed or if the LED light is not working, the front surface can be removed by unscrewing the holding screw on the side of the mounting box that sits between the front surface and the mounting plate. Once this screw is undone, lift the front surface upwards and off, and disconnect the LED cable at the connecting plug. Once the front surface is removed, the LED strip can be inspected for any faults, or the mounting plate can be unscrewed at the four bolts to completely uninstall the artwork.

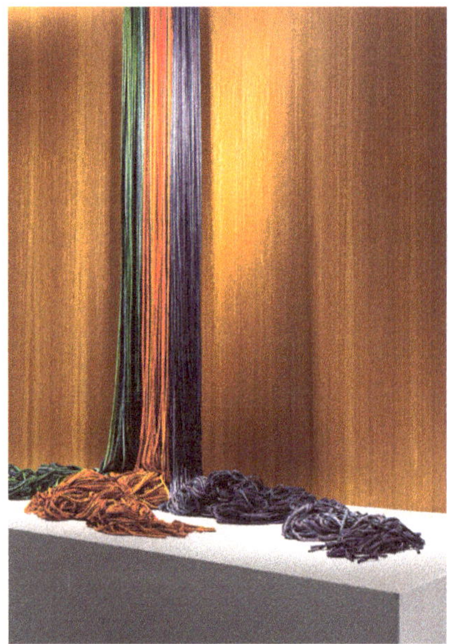

Artist: Anne-Marie May
Instagram: @annemariemay.studio
Location: Melbourne-based artist

Title: Infinity Loop
(oscillating flow), 2020

Material: 3mm tinted
cast acrylic sheet

Acrylic Colour References:
Astari Niagara (brand) Red 101

Approximate Weight
of Sculpture: 3 kg

03 Maintenance Report – Example 3

About the Artwork: Infinity Loop (oscillating flow), 2020, is constructed from a single but complex outline of a shape – a hand-drawn line has been transferred to computer-based architectural software, then laser-cut into coloured translucent acrylic, which takes form according to the inherent properties of the material as the artist applies heat and force to bend and shape the components. This artwork is a result of a complex process born from the simple act of drawing, and the result is a flat plane of material transformed through spatial contortion to become voluminous.

Maintenance: Normal wear and tear. The surface of the acrylic may contain some minor marks and irregularities produced during the process of making. Overall, the artwork surface is in excellent new condition.

Routine Cleaning: Over time, dust will accumulate on the sculpture, so periodically the artwork may require a routine clean. This only needs only to be done as necessary. Regular inspections should be carried out to monitor the artwork's general condition and also determine when cleaning may be necessary.

Cleaning Process:
— To remove dust that has settled on the surface of the sculpture, we recommend using a microfibre cloth as it is very soft and non-abrasive.
— Wearing cotton gloves is recommended to ensure that fingerprints do not mark the artwork. Work on a table with the artwork resting on a piece of fabric.

- To clean the work, use the microfibre cleaning cloth and very gently remove dust on the artwork surface with the cloth. Regularly fold the cloth to ensure a clean area of the cloth is used for each section. Intensive rubbing may cause scratches. Continue the process until complete.
- To remove any residue on the acrylic, use either VuPlex or Kunst-Stoff plastic cleaning products. Periodically applying these products maintains a protective layer on the Perspex. The VuPlex or Kunst-Stoff is applied to dust-free surfaces with a microfibre cloth and then polished back to remove any smearing.

Regular Maintenance Inspections

Having maintenance reports for each of your artworks will ensure your collection can be looked after properly. It is important that the collection be maintained regularly by professional art cleaners every three months (at least), and a cleaning and maintenance report for each quarterly inspection be documented. I suggest this be done by the person who looks after your art collection – whether that's you or someone in your organisation that acts as the collection's curator or done with the help of your art consultant.

Art Register and Insurance

Aside from compiling information and a maintenance manual for each artwork in your collection, I recommend you create an art register that documents each artwork in a simple and clear way. This will be useful for keeping track of what is in the collection, what is added and what is removed (or sold) in the future. The best format for your art register would be an Excel spreadsheet. Remember to keep the information simple and concise.

This information should include:
- the artist's name or names
  (some artists may go by a different name in the public realm)
- the gallery that represents them
- a photograph of the artwork
- a short description of the artwork
- what kind of artwork it is and the medium used, for example:
  a painting, a steel sculpture, a digital installation, etc.
- the year it was acquired for the collection
- the location of the artwork on the site, for example:
  Level 30 by the lift
- the purchase price.

Other notes you could add to each entry include any relevant press, social media or websites that mention the artwork or artist; just remember to update these regularly. You may consider adding some maintenance notes as well if you would like to see these at a glance.

I recommend you keep all the receipts and/or invoices for your artworks as you will need these for insurance purposes. It is vital to have your artwork insured! Make sure that you do this, and if you need help, ask your art consultant how best to go about it.

In addition, your receipts will come in useful for determining resale values if you ever decide to sell an artwork in the collection.

GOLDEN POINTS

01 Develop a vision for your art collection using an art narrative to help you find a key focus and create clear guidelines for what goes into the art collection; this avoids you buying an artwork that doesn't fit your requirements.

02 Choose artworks that are relatable to your business, perhaps something fun and accessible, and engage your staff in artwork choices.

03 Try to establish a wide-ranging collection with works by emerging, mid-tier and established artists.

04 Ensure that each artwork has a plaque that acknowledges the artist.

05 Always insure your art collection!

THE ROAD-BLOCKERS ARE BECOMING RARER & RARER

The road-blockers are becoming rarer and rarer. I can feel a new vanguard emerging: people who are keen to make a social impact, to be involved in creativity and innovation.

ART CONFIDENCE WITHIN THE ORGANISATION

Through our extensive experience at Art Pharmacy, we have found that people have varying levels of art confidence – that is, how much they know about, understand or are interested in art differs. This can affect how they approach their art project.

Before you start your art project, think about what level of art confidence your organisation has and how that might influence your art project. To help you do this, I have identified five categories of organisational interest in art and their respective confidence levels.

01 The Beginner

Incorporating public art into projects is new to this sort of organisation, but once they decide to do it, they want to include art in a thoughtful way. They are usually willing to be guided in their art choices and are open to direction. Their art confidence may be low, but they are willing to learn more so are open to being educated about art.

02 Those with a Thirst for Knowledge

This kind of organisation has some art knowledge and understand that strong public art can make a difference to a development; they are often keen to know more and grow their art confidence. They are willing to engage and invest time, money and resources into finding the right person or team to work on their art project, and want art and culture to become ingrained in their work culture. They have low- to mid-level art confidence but are keen to develop their knowledge further. In these organisations, senior management are often behind the initiative to explore art; they are open to new ideas and want to push boundaries.

03 Those with a Restricted View about Art

While they often know a bit about art and understand the need to include public art in a development project, they are keen to cater to their project in the least expensive and easiest way they can – their budget is their first priority, rather than the artwork. They may have low- to mid-level art confidence but are unlikely to want to go further or take risks. While they still want to deliver a good art project, they prefer to stay on the safer side. In this kind of organisation, the person tasked with the job doesn't usually have a strong interest in art and is not a creative pioneer.

     THE PROJECT TEAM

04 Enthusiastic with Some Knowledge

Some organisations with a good understanding of art throw themselves into an art project but are less willing to accept guidance. This results in a way of working that is not as collaborative as it could be. They may have mid-level confidence but could gain more if they open themselves to possibility. At Art Pharmacy, we try to encourage organisations at this level to think outside the square.

05 Art and Culture Buffs

Some organisations are really engaged in the art scene and have an informed and strong knowledge about what is out there. They look to push boundaries, have fun with their art projects and are often confident enough to suggest artists that may suit. Their people have a high-level of art confidence and are always willing to learn more.

An organisation with any of these levels of art confidence has the potential to support a great art project if they are willing and have the right people on board.

Identifying your organisation's level will help you decide how to approach the task and who to select to manage your project. Having the right person as your art project manager will increase your chances of successful art project implementation and delivery.

THE IN-HOUSE PROJECT TEAM

Every project is different and will have its own set of challenges. Usually, a variety of specialist consultants will be involved with the running and managing of an art project. Depending on the type and complexity of the project, this will likely include the property developer, the architect and the marketing or communications manager. However, because of the many different aspects that are involved in large art projects, there also needs to be a dedicated art project manager: someone who can clearly state what the organisation is looking for and keep everything – and everyone – on track.

As the art project will involve an artist (possibly more than one), I strongly recommend that the art project manager be a person who has an affinity for the arts and who can sympathise with or have empathy for artists and how they work. I can't stress enough how important it is to select the right champion within your organisation to work with the artists and your art consultant (should you choose to employ one). Doing this will be a great help to the overall outcome of the project.

One of our golden rules at Art Pharmacy is that **art always needs to be discussed at the beginning of a great project.** Considerations need to be made early, rather than halfway through or towards the end. That's also where a dedicated art manager comes in.

So, who would fit the bill? Generally, if Art Pharmacy is working with an organisation as their art consultant, we find that people in marketing and communications roles, executives or department heads, community engagement staff or those in cultural or business development teams are best placed to manage the implementation and delivery of creative art projects. Not only are they well versed in the logistics of project management, but they are also able to keep in mind and communicate the intention of the proposed artwork to all levels of their organisation.

People in these roles are usually plugged into the storytelling, or the 'art narrative', behind a new space or project. They may have some understanding of placemaking, and they are well positioned to navigate conceptual outcomes such as engagement and perception (of safety, acceptance, joy, welcome, etc.), and ensure consistency of the art project regarding both the organisation's brand and the community's needs. People in these roles are savvy, and embrace the idea of creating a legacy through experience and engagement via a shared narrative, making them perfect for managing the art project for your development.

TYPES OF PROJECTS

In this section, I have broken down some of the different projects that you might encounter and suggest who within your organisation could be suitable to manage them. However, your needs will depend on your project, so think of this overview as a starting point.

> **Project Type:** Art Strategy Development,
> Public Realm Artwork, Masterplan Developments
> Time Range: 6 — 36 months, depending on scope

These jobs tend to be lengthy and involve many consultants, anywhere from ten to 50, including architects, landscape architects, engineers, councils, flooding specialists, project developers, leasing managers and marketing managers ... the list of who can be involved goes on. These jobs are usually high-profile and require patience because of the number of consultants that will need to be managed. They are usually taken care of by a dedicated art project manager, or a contractor from the architect's team whose sole role is to keep everyone on track.

Project Type: Lobby and Community Activations
Time Range: usually temporary, running between
two and 12 months

Lobby artworks or activations are usually managed by marketing, asset, partnership, property or communication managers. The aim of the work is to engage the tenants of the property. With a relatively quick turnaround cycle, the desired outcome of these art projects is for the art to focus on the community and culture of the building, and for art to bring the tenants together in an inclusive way. The art is there for all to enjoy.

At Art Pharmacy, we have also seen a move by the property sector towards improving the health and wellbeing of tenancy communities, especially in the metropolitan and CBD areas. Some examples of this initiative include lobby activations installed to coincide with cultural events including Mardi Gras, Sustainability Week, Lunar New Year, NAIDOC Week, International Women's Day and Wellbeing Week. In some instances, workshops were also held to create awareness around these cultural events.

Project Type: Creation and Management
of a Corporate Art Collection
Time Range: 3 – 18 months, sometimes longer,
sometimes ongoing

The management of corporate art collections differs a little to the development of an art project for a new or refurbished space. It is often undertaken by people in the client service, service delivery or operations areas – anyone who looks after clients and customers coming to visit the space. These collections are usually about the company and their brand, values or mission statement, what they want to communicate and how they are perceived by visitors to the space.

In addition, sometimes a new office or a refurbishment of an existing office will warrant new artworks. Art Pharmacy has acted as consultants on these types of projects several times, often being engaged when a business moves premises. From our experiences in this area, we have found that if the facility manager or client service manager is connected with what the partners of the corporate building want for the collection, and understand the needs of people who visit the site, the outcome is usually positive and the process becomes an integral brand exercise.

GOLDEN POINTS

01 Determine your organisation's level of art confidence before starting the project.

02 Decide what type of art project is right for your organisation – public realm artwork, lobby or community activation, or a corporate art collection.

03 Having the right art project manager is key to your project's success – choose someone with an affinity for the arts who will champion the project.

Assessing Levels of Art Appreciation

To help select the person who will manage your art project, it is useful to gauge who in your team has an interest in art. When Art Pharmacy works with an organisation, we often do this through an exercise that involves getting a group of relevant staff together, perhaps ten or more, and asking them the following questions:

- Who buys art for their home?
- Who has been to an art gallery lately?
- Who visits galleries or museums when they travel?
- Who does a creative hobby? What is that hobby?
- Does anyone have an artist, actor or a musician in the family?
- Does anyone attend the theatre?
- Who thinks it is important that their children do art or another creative hobby?

These questions open up conversation and it is easy to get an understanding of everyone's level of art knowledge and engagement. We learn who loves art and who might work well with an artist, which helps us identify who might be interested in taking on the role of the art manager of the project.

This exercise is a fun and productive way of instigating new learnings for your team. It takes around 30 to 45 minutes and is usually put to a group of people in the same project team or department. The questions are designed to encourage and support the participants, so no answer is wrong. What we find is that often there are one or two people in the room who have artworks hanging in their homes, or who buy from art fairs or galleries. Most people will have been to an art gallery recently. The personal stories that emerge are great for building team dynamics and deciding who is best placed to be your art project manager.

We've been surprised by this exercise in the past. We once put these questions to a room of 25 members of a large property developer's wider team. In that group, we had one person say that they couldn't answer in the affirmative in any way to any of the questions – not even one! There was some awkward laughter in the room when we discovered that this person oversaw developing a precinct-wide, long-term art strategy for one of the state's largest new communities. I can't tell you how devastating this discovery was for us. This individual was unlikely to have the right knowledge to brief artists or define projects or be comfortable in providing the feedback that shapes an art project towards a successful outcome.

This example is one of the reasons why I am writing this book. My aim is to educate organisations, developers and council workers; to encourage them to select the right person to steer and champion their creative project; someone who has a passion for and an interest in art. This is the only way to create a successful and meaningful art project.

Picking the Right Champion

Given the above example, it is imperative that you pick the right champion for your art project. The person who is responsible for managing an art project must have some level of comfort, knowledge or experience with art, or they must be able to appoint a more knowledgeable team member who does. If you don't have someone like this in your team, then you may need to hire an expert consultancy group who can provide you with an art consultant.

Establishing how comfortable your decision-makers are with art is also key if you are attempting to commission unique projects under management that has historically seemed to 'not get it' or has been conservative and risk-averse during creative projects. This is when projects can get a bit stuck. In these cases, it is useful to establish your organisation's track record on previous creative projects. Knowing what has or hasn't gone well in the past will help inform how you approach a new project. If you can, find out who managed a previous art project/s and speak to them about their experiences. What did they learn? What did they need to outsource? What details and tips can they pass on to you?

The nature of working in large organisations can make this sometimes difficult to establish, so we always encourage our clients to document this type of information for each art project they do. This will enable them to share their experiences as well as learn from them in the future.

If there is no information to hand, I recommend that those new to art project management start small with a low-risk temporary project. This means they can work out the kinks in the art project process and gain feedback from managers and stakeholders before they embark on a big permanent piece, or an expensive and public activation. It is important that if mistakes are made or wobbles are experienced, these happen without a loss of face or the wasting of money and time. No one wants a PR disaster on their hands!

To help do this, you could consider tracking what others are doing in similar spaces – but it is important to be aware that it is not useful to use the same artists others have used or copy someone else's art strategy. This is not best practice and will not be a good look for your brand or the project. Unfortunately, I have seen this happen many times.

In a contrast to the example of the art project manager who had virtually no knowledge of art, we have been fortunate to work with people who, while having limited experience with art and artists, had a strong passion for or interest in both. This really does change the overall temperament of the project and the likelihood of its success. Those who are passionate, who champion the project, are more likely to deliver a successful outcome.

     THE PROJECT TEAM

We call this kind of person a 'creative pioneer' – they're ready and willing to support what art can do for their organisation.

In addition, we have found that after the budding creative pioneer successfully delivers an art project for the first time, the experience they've gained gives them something tangible to be proud of, akin to a personal legacy, and they grow their confidence. This is often a sweet victory they are happy to share and are keen to experience again.

For larger projects such as masterplan developments, it is possible that your art manager – your budding creative pioneer – will need a sounding board to confirm the direction of the art. If so, then it is useful to set up an art committee. This would function as an advisory panel and consist of a small group of people who can offer support to the art project manager, and act as an extension of them. In these cases, the project manager and the art committee work together to get the right outcome.

GOLDEN POINTS

01 Assess your and the team's level of art appreciation using the exercise included in this chapter.

02 Pick someone who has some level of comfort, knowledge or experience with art to be your art project manager. If they have a passion for or interest in art, they will better champion your art project and may even become a creative pioneer!

03 If undertaking a larger project, consider forming an art committee to assist and support the art project manager.

04 Try a smaller win before taking on a large project to test your and your team's ability to work in the creative sector.

EMPOWERING THE CREATIVE PIONEER

At Art Pharmacy, we work with a wide range of people and find that many have a profound and deep interest in art, while others have only a little. Gauging people's interest in art is part of our job. Some clients start with a slight interest, but once they know what art can offer their project outcome, they are keen to know more. If they then go on to manage an art project and experience some success with it, their art confidence grows and they may become passionate about championing art in their organisation. With a little encouragement, these committed art implementers grow into creative pioneers.

I touched on this idea in *Making Art Matter* and it's vitally important for people to champion art and artists with those around them. It can make an enormous difference to artists, organisations and the broader community.

Art Education and the Creative Pioneer

I sometimes wonder about the intersection between art education and entrepreneurship. Many artists who have gone to art school have not been trained in the commercial reality of being an artist. They're sometimes ill-prepared for what the world has to offer them. In the early days of Art Pharmacy, I used to send out template invoices and explain how to get an ABN to some artists. Sometimes I still do. While it is easy to support learning about art and culture in the early years of a child's education, when it gets to the high school stage, students interested in art may not always be encouraged to follow a creative path. There is a general perception that a career in art is not entirely viable. I think this may partly come down to artists not being taught how to run their practice as a business, even at a tertiary level of education.

Due to the way careers in art have been perceived, there are many people out there with a profound love for art and culture, people who may have studied art at school but have ended up doing other jobs. You could possibly be one of those people! These secret artists have the potential to be excellent creative pioneers.

Creative pioneers are everywhere in our society, often hidden away in roles you wouldn't expect. They may be accountants, engineers, lawyers or business owners. I meet them all the time. Deep down, a creative pioneer might have once wanted to be an artist, singer or actor, but perhaps felt that the arts might not offer them a stable career; but because of their love for the arts, they may feel empowered to become a creative pioneer. As these passionate people learn how to work with artists and others in the creative industries, and the more they are encouraged to do so by the people around them, the greater confidence they'll have in developing and implementing art projects and commissioning artists.

Through supporting the arts, these creative pioneers can explore their own creativity and build relationships with the artistic tribe they've always wanted to belong to.

Creative pioneers can also play a role in supporting others who support the arts. Many arts workers are often the only person in their team involved in an art project. This can sometimes mean they are stretched across many tasks and don't have a creative and supportive network around them. Creative pioneers can serve as an advocate for these workers on creative projects, supporting them in their sometimes difficult roles. At Art Pharmacy, we feel fortunate because many of these creative pioneers support what we do.

If you think you would like to be a creative pioneer in your workplace, or recognise someone who might be, I suggest you first think about the values and intention of your organisation and how it uses art in projects. If there is already a staff member or a team that values art and culture, think about learning from them so you can build your confidence. Gauge your level of art confidence through completing the exercises mentioned earlier in this chapter. If a role comes up for an art project manager, put yourself forward, or talk to that colleague you know who loves art and encourage them to have a go. Having a love of art will put you ahead of others for the job and your enthusiasm will energise those you work with.

As you navigate this new role, remember to work with those around you in a respectful and productive way. If you engage an art consultant, think of the relationship you'll build with them as a collaborative one. Art consultants are creative pioneers too, and work hard to support the artists they deal with. They can guide you in supporting the creative community in the best and most effective way.

What Makes a Fully Fledged Creative Pioneer?

Once you have embraced supporting the arts, you'll soon find that art, culture, creativity and innovation will become core values for you – meaning you'll have become a fully fledged creative pioneer. These creative pioneers strive to be authentic and to support the creative community. They are ready to take things to the next level.

Fully fledged creative pioneers:
- are curious and interested, host events, arrange tours and invite speakers to share knowledge with their organisation
- speak up when they want to do something or drive change in management, and encourage staff to engage with art and creativity
- continually champion artists, creatives and art organisations, and always do so with respect

　　　THE PROJECT TEAM

    – are leaders who are open to and welcoming of new ideas,
and encourage all staff to contribute to the exploration
of art in the organisation
    – support culturally and linguistically diverse (CALD) artists,
First Nations artists and artists from other diverse backgrounds.

The Art and Culture Economy

Artists and creatives should be empowered in our local economy; however, the arts sector consists of a secretive bunch. Many in the arts are protective of the way they do things. It is an unregulated industry without any real process documents or specific, common standards to work to. One of my aims in writing this book is to show people how the creative industry can be bolstered by those in business who love art and have the power to support it. I'm keen to get people supporting the arts, even if that means encouraging one creative pioneer at a time!

Knowing how best to support the art and culture economy is about education and empowerment. All of us need to be advocates for the creative industries. We have the power to shift the way we, and our organisations, think about art and the creative community, and we can do this in an authentic way.

There are many people and companies who already support and appreciate art, but others might not know how to take the next step. That's OK; being involved in supporting the creative community is about starting small and giving it a go. It's about being curious and willing to learn, and having a desire to work through things together.

Culture Starts at the Top

While it's important for creative pioneers to be present across various levels within an organisation, it is vital that their passion be taken up by the organisation's CEO and managing directors. If those at senior level are not participating in discussions around ways of supporting the arts with their creative pioneers, it will be hard for pioneers to feel empowered to push for change.

The creative pioneer may feel like they have the weight of expectation on them. Therefore, it is important for them to have support, or another creative pioneer to work with, at management level. Your organisation will have a much more authentic experience with their art projects – whether that be in commissioning art or building a collection – if management also appreciates the arts. In my experience, I have found that this appreciation for arts and culture is likely to then filter down from the top through the entire organisation.

Having someone at management level waving the creative pioneer flag will help your organisation develop a strong and lasting relationship with art. And if there isn't anyone currently in management who could fit the bill, let me assure you that managers can be influenced to become creative pioneers! Change can be on the horizon for them – they just need an opportunity to think about their relationship to art.

If you are in a mid-tier or even an entry-level position in your organisation and are keen on being a creative pioneer, then my suggestion is to find someone in management who is like-minded and who loves art – someone who you can affiliate yourself with to grow the organisation's involvement in art projects. Being involved in the arts is a collaborative adventure; together, you and management, can make a big social impact by supporting the creative community.

How to Promote Change

I have found that in some organisations the 'old guard' may not quite understand the idea of people wanting to be creative pioneers or art implementers. They may even block those seeking change, especially if they're attached to an old style of leadership or if they have no real interest in art. These people are often dubious about new ideas and may not have a good understanding about the creative community. They are also unlikely to grasp the importance of art to developments or corporate offices. Fostering the arts may not have been something that was encouraged in their early days in business, so is not part of their core values.

In my time dealing with corporate art projects, I have heard many throw-away comments from senior management about artists and artwork that have been shocking and sometimes offensive. I believe that these comments come from people with a certain mindset, one which needs to be reconsidered and changed. There are still some road-blockers out there in senior management and on boards who are not interested in social impact or the community. Often, these people are focused only on the dollar value of a project. They enjoy their position of authority and believe their way is the only way.

Mindset

In these cases, try to do your best to change their mindset. Put forward your thoughts in a constructive way, show them the importance of art and the outcomes it can produce and work to sell them the idea of being a creative pioneer. However, if you have done everything you can and are still coming up against a brick wall, and you are still determined to advocate for the arts in your workplace, then you may need to think about a new role somewhere else.

Sometimes, moving on and finding another organisation that will support you and your vision is the only answer. I encourage you to find that place where your creative pioneering spirit is supported by like-minded people who are part of your tribe. Culture starts at the top and filters down; if it is simply too hard to change the mindset of your management, think about moving on.

The New Vanguard

The road-blockers are becoming rarer and rarer. I can feel a new vanguard emerging; people who are keen to make a social impact, to be involved in creativity and innovation.

Appreciation of the arts is on the rise. If you are a creative pioneer, there are organisations out there waiting for someone like you. The more people who want art as part of their working life, the bigger the win for the creative community.

GOLDEN POINTS

01 There are budding creative pioneers everywhere. With a little support and encouragement from those around them, they can become fully fledged art champions who implement art within their organisation.

02 Some people may not wave the creative pioneer flag, but there is a new generation emerging who are keen for social change and understand how art can help them make an impact. Don't be scared to gather support from those around you to help you talk to your managers.

Passion and Peer Level

In my first book *Making Art Matter* I talked about how important it is that you have passion for your project. That means your dedicated art project manager should, ideally, also have a passion for it. However, it is equally important that they be capable of executing the delivery of the project – that they have enough experience to manage what will be involved and are on a level with their peers where they can make the required decisions to keep the project moving from start to finish.

In the past, I have seen some organisations think it appropriate to appoint graduate students with less than a year of experience as their art project manager. This can be hard work on several accounts – for the art consultant (if one is employed) and for the graduate, who must try to understand the landscape of internal politics within the organisation, is given little or no leeway to make decisions and has little or no experience in project management. While some can thrive under these conditions, I believe art projects should be led by someone with at least senior-level project management skills. My recommendation is for the prospective art manager to have been with the organisation for at least 18 to 24 months. Engaging someone of this skill level will be highly beneficial to the health, delivery and outcome of the project.

From our view as outside consultants, we can tell how an organisation sees the art project by who they appoint as the art manager.

Junior or Recent Graduate

If a graduate is selected, we feel that the organisation isn't serious about art. A graduate fresh from university does not have a voice within the organisation. Asking them to be responsible for the art project really isn't best practice; it says the organisation is using art as a box to tick.

Someone Who Lacks Passion for Art

If the art project manager does not have an interest in art, we know their job is just to deliver the project at hand. While they're important for delivering the job, their mindset isn't conducive to getting the best outcome on the art project.

Someone Who Lacks Influence in the Organisation

This tends to happen quite frequently. While the chosen art manager may have a strong interest in art and the project, they may not have the power or creative influence in their organisation to make a difference. It is important to have an art champion who can make the project happen.

At Art Pharmacy, we always seek to work with people within the organisation who have a strategic business mindset and a passion for art, and who are on a peer level with us. For anyone choosing an art manager for an art project, these characteristics should be essential requirements in any potential candidate.

Project Completion End to End

So, in addition to selecting a person who is passionate about art and familiar with storytelling and community engagement to be your art project manager, that person should also be well placed to manage the project from start to finish. Running an art project isn't easy. The person you choose should be aware there will be many tasks they'll need to juggle. Your art project manager will need to:

- identify the purpose of the project
- identify some possible sites for art placement
- develop an art narrative for the project
- help you work out a budget
- create a longlist of artists for you to select from and help you cull this to a shortlist
- develop a brief for the artist to work to that includes concept direction
- help you choose and finalise the design concept that will be made into an artwork
- liaise with the artist/s
- organise contracts for the artist/s
- create and manage the project's timeline
- organise a photographer and videographer to document the artwork
- organise installation day, including organising work health and safety (WHS) documents and maintenance reports
- be confident when speaking with architects, site managers and engineers
- help the marketing department to publicise the project, including using the photography and videography that has been commissioned.

While your project manager will have assistance for some of these tasks, they will still need to be able to deliver the project successfully, get everyone on board at the right time (including the artists) and follow the budget and timeline. Therefore, they should be at a level where they can make decisions and where people in the organisation will listen to them. They'll need to have a clear vision of the roadmap to installation and actively consider the associated parallel planning for the project.

If you can't identify someone within your organisation who you think can do this successfully, then you should consider getting in an external art consultant.

02 ART CONFIDENCE

01 THE RIGHT TEAM

03 THE ART STRATEGY

04 BUDGET, COPYRIGHT & LICENSING

06 ARTIST BRIEF

05 CREATING AN ART NARRATIVE

07 SOURCING AN ARTIST

08 DESIGN CONCEPTS & DIRECTIONS

10 CONTRACTS

09 SELECTING THE ARTIST

11 INSTALLATION & POST INSTALLATION DEBRIEF

12 TROUBLE-SHOOTING

14 MARKETING & AUDIENCE ENGAGEMENT

13 THE CREATION OF A LEGACY

15 THE LIFETIME OF THE ARTWORK

16 THE IMPACT OF ART

Key Person Risk

While we recommend having a dedicated art project manager, there is something else to keep in mind for your art project: key person risk. Having only one person to look after everything can be a risk if that person leaves the organisation or can no longer look after the project. If your project is large, such as a masterplan development, then once the project gets the go ahead, we encourage enlisting at least one other person who will be across everything that relates to the art project – in effect, a two-person minimum. So, that's two people within your organisation or business who will be familiar with the project from day one, just to be safe. And if you can have more, that will only benefit the outcome.

When I was working for a large hotel in Sydney, for example, halfway through the job the development manager moved interstate. Fortunately, we had their assistant on board, and they ended up managing the project with us. Since they had been part of the process from the very beginning, they knew what needed to be done and we didn't lose too much time.

It is critical on large, longer masterplan developments that you accept and expect the possibility of staff changes. By taking key person risk into account early on, you'll save your project and your organisation's integrity. An art committee that supports the art project manager can also function as a backup to cover risk.

GOLDEN POINTS

01 Select a project manager with an appreciation of arts and culture. This person will be your art champion. With an enthusiasm for art, they will support and manage the project through the various roadblocks you may encounter.

02 Ensure that the person running the project can make necessary decisions to keep the project moving or has a connection with the decision-makers in your organisation.

03 To cover key person risk, make sure there are at least two people who are across the project – that means if your key person leaves, you'll have a backup.

THE EXTERNAL ART CONSULTANT
If you are unable to find the right person in your organisation for the role of art project manager, or if your project is large and requires managing many different elements and people at once, you may wish to consider employing an external art consultant or curator to manage your art project. In this section, we look at how to select an external person that will best fit your project and your organisation.

Being involved in the arts is a collaborative adventure; together, you and management can make a big social impact by supporting the creative community.

The Art World

The commercial art world can be daunting to navigate for the uninitiated. The industry is not well defined and trying to identify standard practices can sometimes seem fruitless. There is huge variation in the way art consultants, curators, gallery owners and independent art agents define projects, align incentives and charge for their services.

Due to the competitive and secretive nature of this world, I believe commissioning bodies can often end up feeling confused about what they are paying for. I have been brought in at the late stage of a number of projects after the relationship between the commissioning body and their art consultant/art curator/artist has broken down. Sadly, it is the artist who is often left in the lurch with a career-making project off the cards after months of work. So, it is important for both you and your organisation – and the artist you will eventually work with – to find the right art consultant for your project.

Like any industry, the art world has specialist areas. Even after working in the industry for over 20 years, I am still learning about new roles and how they intersect with existing ones. These roles include art historians and professors, art valuers and restorers, art PR, independent and institutional curators, independent artists and craft makers, fabricators (from steel workers to stonemasons) and sculptors. Subsections of the art world include art foundations, art copyright agencies, NFT agencies that work with digital artworks, international and national art fairs, art education (secondary school, college and university level), public art, regional and national galleries, commercial galleries, art prizes and arts funding.

Given these many art roles and areas, it is easy to see how confusing, specialist and complex the art world can be, especially if you are new to working with it. Employing an art consultant will help you navigate this world as you work on your art project. Even so, I recommend that you have a dedicated internal person who will work with the external art consultant you choose. While this person will not manage the art project itself, they will be the key point of contact for the art consultant to ensure the project keeps moving forward.

When choosing this person, consider the same points you would when looking for an internal art project manager. Keep in mind that this contact person should be at a peer level with the external consultant so that decisions on the project can be made quickly and accurately along the way. They should also be able to gauge your organisation's level of art confidence and communicate this to your consultant, as this will help the consultant understand what you will need.

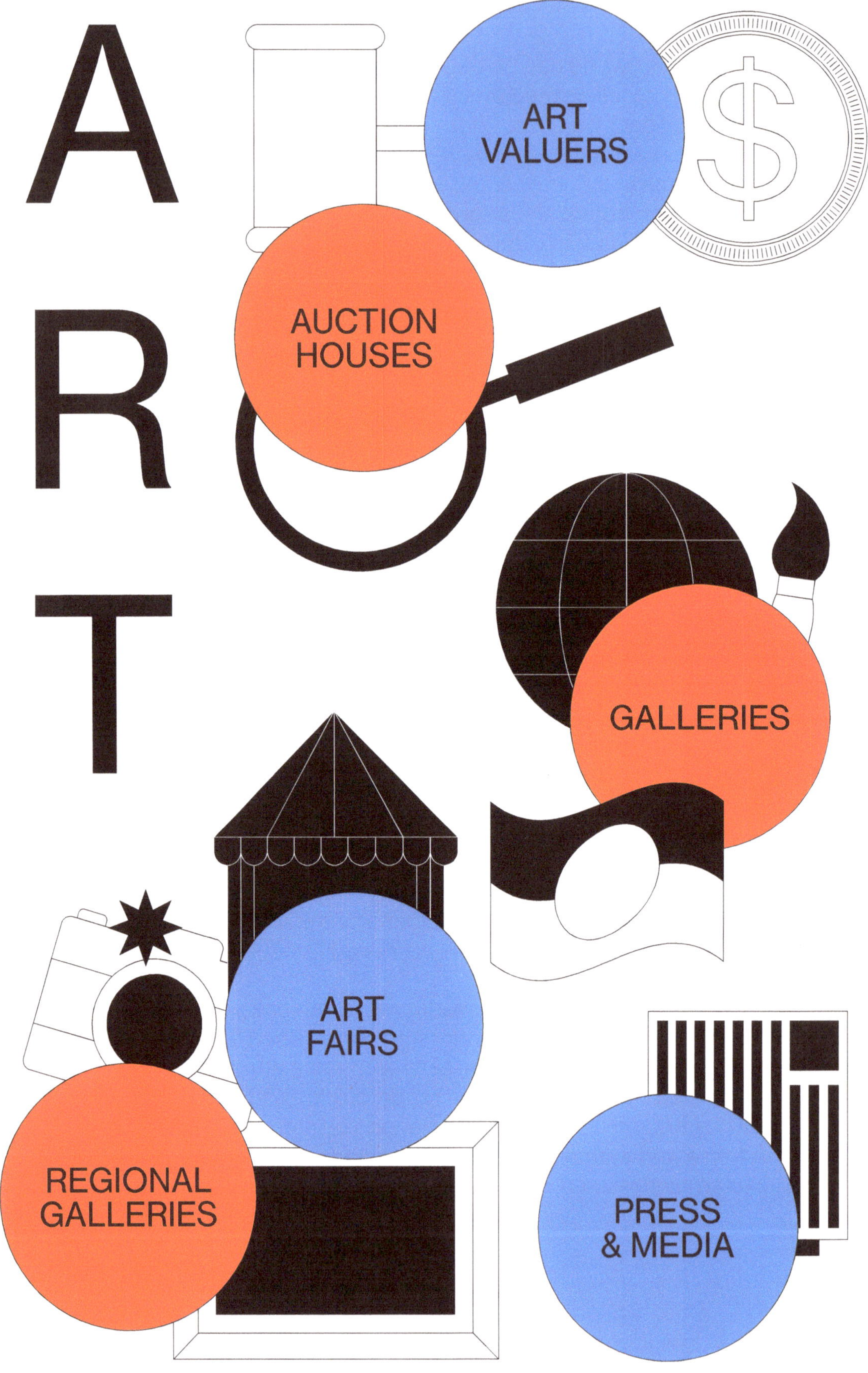

A
R
T
ART VALUERS
AUCTION HOUSES
GALLERIES
ART FAIRS
REGIONAL GALLERIES
PRESS & MEDIA

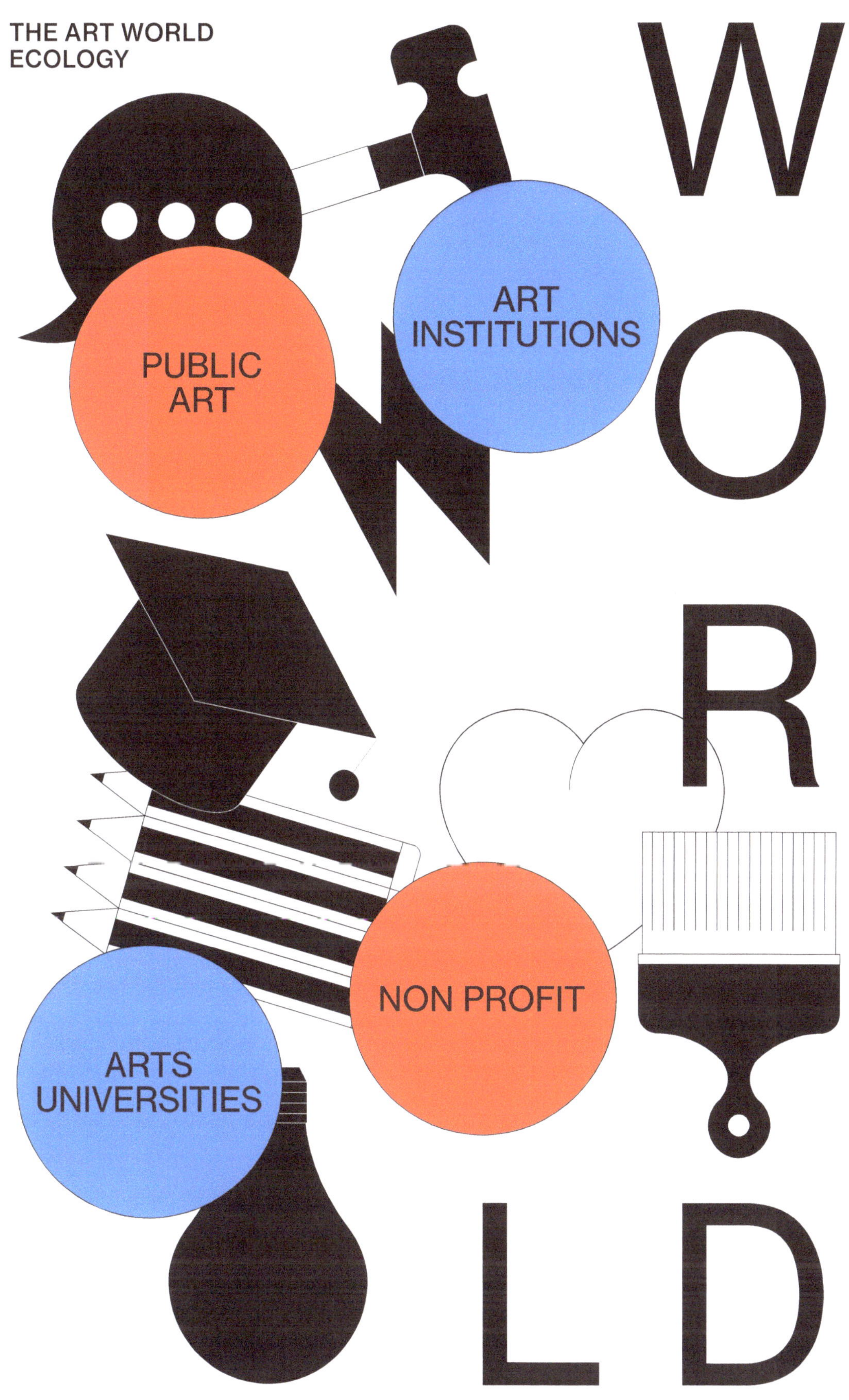
PUBLIC
ART
ART
INSTITUTIONS
NON PROFIT
ARTS
UNIVERSITIES
W
O
R
L
D

Picking the Consultant that is Right for You

Any external art consultant you choose will play a huge role in the success of the project, so it is important that you and your consultant understand each other. Finding the right consultant is a bit like dating. This is a really important point and something you should think of as a philosophy. When making your choice, have a think about what your art likes and dislikes are, and how wild or restricted you want to be with the project.

Then when you first meet your prospective art consultant, assess what their values are and work out if they align to yours. Like on any first date, check out the synergies between you.

As large projects can be anywhere between two and 36 months in duration, it is important that you can see yourself working with your consultant for that length of time. This works both ways; at Art Pharmacy, we have turned away several projects because we couldn't see a long-term future with them. If your synergies don't align, why work together?

My advice here is to know what you want and ask lots of questions in that initial meeting. Art consultants work in different ways, and some specialise in different areas, such as corporate or private collections. They may work with local artists or specialise in international artists. They may represent a stable of artists and have exclusive agreements with them, or they may be an agent for a gallery and will take a percentage of the artist's fee.

While there is nothing inherently wrong with the art consultant being an agent for a gallery, it can become a little confusing and complicated when it comes to fees. When working in this way, fees are often communicated as percentages and commission, while other tasks are itemised through detailed scopes. Sometimes this can lead to incorrect assumptions being made about what the consultant's role is.

It is important to understand the difference in the way art consultants might work. Think about what you like and prefer before you meet with likely candidates.

ART DATING

So, we now know that finding a consultant that you have a synergy
with is important. At Art Pharmacy, the way we look at how we develop
relationships with our clients really is like dating. There will be some clients
who are enthusiastic, willing to learn and keen to put in the effort and time
required to understand how art can benefit their projects. They want
to build their art confidence. We see these as long-term relationships
with lots of potential – a bit like a marriage.

Others will be keen to learn but might outgrow the relationship we have
with them. These are more like boyfriends/girlfriends/significant others –
they could be mid-term or long-term, but the relationship will probably wind
down at some point. It ends amicably with both parties as friends who are
happy to meet up every now and then.

On the other end of the scale, there are some clients that might be
considered to be flings. For various reasons, things just don't work out.
We've found it's best to avoid these relationships as they won't last.

While I'm presenting these from an art consultant's point of view, if
you are a commissioning body or an art project manager thinking about
employing an art consultant, you too will need to consider how you want
to develop the relationship you have with them. Your dating preference
will come down to your art values and whether art is important to your
organisation. The outline here on the various art relationships you might
have also applies to how you work with your team and the artist who will
create your project's artwork. I encourage you to apply what we have
learnt at Art Pharmacy to your own art relationships.

Marriage Clients

We always strive to build our clients into marriage material.
Marriage clients are enjoyable to work with and are
comfortable with collaborative teamwork. We can each pick
up the phone at a moment's notice and work together to
solve any problem in an art project. We can work honestly
and openly with one another.

Marriage clients understand that art is important. Like any
marriage, our relationship with these clients is based upon
shared goals, compatibility and a common vision of the world
and the future. We both benefit from an open and collaborative
relationship. This is the type of relationship that produces
great art results.

Boyfriend/Girlfriend/Significant Other

These kinds of art relationships are similar to what we have with marriage clients, but they may change over time. They begin as fun, challenging and interesting; however, after a few years, each party may develop new interests or grow in different directions. While this is a positive relationship, eventually we may both agree that we want different outcomes. If we have grown apart, this type of relationship might naturally dissolve, with both parties generally remaining friends. We are always happy to work with these clients when they call us, as we've loved helping them develop their art confidence.

For those looking for an art consultant, this sort of relationship could work if you are testing the waters of art projects.

Flings

Occasionally, we have short-term flings with clients who say they have an interest in art but are unwilling to commit to a long-term strategy. There is no real future with this type of client. Generally, they won't really want to fully engage with art – including it in their project is a tick-the-box process for them. Art wasn't their thing in the first place, but they knew it would increase foot traffic and give a 'cool factor' to their development or space. While we try hard to build art awareness in these clients, we prefer to avoid them.

I've included these examples here to illustrate that these relationships work both ways. If you aren't committed tothe project, your relationship with your art consultant may not blossom the way you would like it to. Remember to think about what you want from the project before you hire someone external to work with you.

Responsibilities of an Art Consultant

It is vital that both you and the art consultant are aware of what will need to be done for the project. The art consultant must be confident they can meet your expectations and deliver what you need.

It is also important that your art consultant be involved from the beginning of the project. They will need to regularly liaise with you or your organisation's dedicated point of contact throughout the project. They will need to have the power to manage the art committee or art panel (if you decide to create one). Part of this relationship will include the art consultant taking on thoughtful and constructive feedback from you, the committee and/or stakeholders when required and relaying this feedback to the artist/s involved in the project.

In the early stages, the art consultant will provide you with a list of diverse artists that meet the project's brief and/or narrative. For each artist listed, they'll include the artist's credentials, a biography of their experience and background, and photographs of previous works. This will give you, the commissioning body, an overview of each candidate and their work.

Once you and your art committee have selected an artist, the consultant will be responsible for drawing up a legal agreement or contract between your organisation and the artist. They will also manage this contract throughout the project and ensure the relevant progress payments are made to the artist.

Your art consultant will ensure the artist's brief is clear, and that both the organisation and the artist know what is expected from answering that brief. Once the artist puts forward some design concepts in response to the brief, the art consultant will then be responsible for managing the delivery of the concepts, along with all the relevant information, in a presentation to stakeholders. They will also need to manage any subsequent revisions or amendments if required.

When these have been agreed on, the art consultant will become responsible for the more practical aspects of the job as well. Your external art consultant should have the ability to work on an art strategy document for the development application (DA) if one is required. They will need to manage drawings and architectural plans, and be aware of your organisation's safety management system, Safe Work Method Statement (SWMS), traffic management plan, production schedule and COVID-19 safety plan.

Part of this will include the art consultant ensuring that the materials used in the artwork meet safety guidelines. For example, the use of non-toxic materials, such as non-toxic paints, is always preferable.

When the artwork creation is underway, the art consultant will manage, if required, any visits to the artist's studio. They will also visit fabricators and organise visits to the development site for the production team. They'll manage timelines with the internal and external team (including builders and other specialists); collate all information for the project's implementation, delivery and installation; and be on top of any other work that needs to be done post-installation, such as arranging the making and installation of content plaques.

Understanding Fees and Deliverables

Understanding how an art consultant works, and how they charge for their work, is another consideration to keep in mind when you make your choice. In any fee proposal, I think it is important for art consultants to articulate their scope. For this reason, at Art Pharmacy we prefer to structure project management fees using an hourly rate, and we outline how many hours are applied to specific project tasks. For example, we break up our fees in stages that clearly articulate to the client what we are doing and show the costs associated with each stage. As many of our clients work to production schedules and milestones, showing our process in this way gives everyone involved the ability to plan timelines.

In addition, you may like to see your consultant break up the project in a sequence of phases, so it is easier to see the progress of the work and the responsibilities they will take on. This will allow for quality control, and both you and the art consultant can ensure that the artist's intent is respected throughout the entire process.

We often break up projects in the following way:

01 Phase 1: Identification of the placement of art within the space; development of an art narrative; and development of an art strategy document that can be taken to council.

02 Phase 2: Presentation of an artist longlist, artist selection and briefing, presentation and finalisation of design concepts for the artwork.

03 Phase 3: Management of artwork production, delivery and installation; execution of any post-installation work.

At Art Pharmacy, in some cases we have been invited to present a list of artists, then to work with the selected artist up to the concept stage, at which point we hand over to the client for them to work with the artist directly. If that is the case, we charge accordingly.

If your art consultant is moving off the project at this stage, they should guide you through formalising the agreement with the artist, including the writing of a suitable contract, and provide you with a clear and detailed handover with suggestions on how to manage the artist. This step is very important as here is where things can get a bit grey, and where an artist's expectations (set by the consultant) may not match your own. Making sure this step is professionally handled will realign everyone's expectations and ensure all involved know what needs to be done. We recommend a face-to-face meeting for this stage so all parties can go over these important details together.

 THE PROJECT TEAM

Alternatively, you might prefer that your consultant takes you on the journey from the beginning to the completion of the project in one outline. This is the ideal option, but the end choice is up to you.

Whichever way you go, it is important that you and your art consultant understand who will take responsibility for each aspect of the project. There may be some elements of the project they cannot deliver for you, so these must be identified early on to avoid aspects of the project being missed, or unexpected additional fees being incurred that are not accounted for in the project's budget.

In all of Art Pharmacy's quotes and proposals, we outline what we deliver and what is out of scope. For instance, we talk about how many concepts will be delivered by the artist and how many amendments our costings cover. It would be good for you to ask your prospective art consultant whether, after delivery of concepts and production of the artwork, they will also be involved in the installation process, and if they can do a maintenance report for the artwork. While these should be part of what they do, some consultants may consider these aspects of the job outside their scope and will charge an additional fee for the work.

For Art Pharmacy, itemising our tasks for our clients makes our scope clearer and easier to evaluate. And because we work with many different artists, from those who are unrepresented and emerging to those who are established and internationally renowned, we prefer not to work with complex commission arrangements with third and fourth parties the way that some consultants who work as agents to galleries do. This keeps things simple for us. We have structured our process to be in line with the way project managers on construction sites work to make it easy for our clients, from developers to councils, to understand how we operate.

How Does the Consultant Select their Artists?

I've already mentioned the possibly confusing fees that result from consultants who act as agents for galleries, but there are also a few things to take into consideration with those who directly represent artists. For example, do they have a regular stable of artists, or do they select and propose unrepresented artists? How do they make their selections?

A consultant might be able to give you a free list of artists for you to choose from, but this is really a cookie-cutter response to an art project. A consultant who does this is likely to have a small stable of artists that they regularly represent. They probably have an agreement or contract with each. While this method is quick and free – a bit like a fling in art dating – it may not be the best way to approach a project if you want a distinctive and memorable result. If your project requires a more thoughtful artist selection – perhaps you are interested in artists that have ties to the location, or you would like to see a diverse list of candidates – a handpicked selection would suit your project better. You might find that an art consultant who represents emerging artists could cater to your project's narrative more closely, particularly if you are looking to stand out from the crowd.

So, if you and your art consultant aren't quite ready for marriage and don't want to commit to the full art project together, then this mid-level relationship will at least provide you with a strong beginning for your art project.

   THE PROJECT TEAM

GOLDEN POINTS

01 The art world is complex. Employing the right art consultant is paramount to the success of your art project.

02 Be open, clear and honest with your consultant about your level of art confidence and experience. They can help you build on it and show you how art can benefit your project.

03 Think about what kind of relationships you want to build with your art consultant, your art team and/or the artist you work with. Work towards marriage or long-term relationships and avoid short-term flings.

ARCHITECTS AND ART CONSULTANTS

Another way that an art consultant may become involved in a project is through the project's architect. I have found that many architecture firms win projects through the tender process and then go on to employ an art consultant to take responsibility for the artwork and placemaking aspects of the project. That is, the architect and art consultant work together in a collaborative way. These are usually good relationships – many architects I know draw and paint, attend art galleries and purchase art. There is a synergy between architecture, design and art.

However, there is a difference between the art consultant who is engaged directly through the architect and the art consultant who is engaged directly by the client.

In the first case, the commissioning body – that's you, the client – will engage the architectural firm, either through tender or directly. The architectural firm will then contract subconsultants, including the art consultant.

In the second case, the commissioning body will engage their art project manager directly, whether that be someone in-house or an external art consultant. If it is an external person or consultancy, this is also done either directly or by tender. The architect is not generally involved in this choice. Instead, they will be expected to work side by side with the art consultant.

Considerations

If the architect is responsible for selecting the art consultant, that is one less job for you, as the commissioning body, to consider. You are giving the architect full control of what artworks will be included on your site and allowing them to collaborate with their art consultant on the overall design of the art placement.

We have found that there is a growing trend for clients to work directly with the architect, who then employs an art consultant. Many architects now seem to take on more of a project manager role, looking after engineering teams, playground designers, skate park designers and others. On some projects, there can be up to 50 subcontractors on the job, depending on its complexity. From the art project perspective, there are pluses and minuses to this approach.

Pluses

If the architect has won the job by tender, or is employed directly to manage the overall project, the time-consuming processes between council or government organisations are streamlined. The architect becomes responsible for the management of the entire team of consultants, including the art consultant. They become a one-stop shop.

Also, architects tend to know about art, meaning they are likely to have a good understanding of the art project for the site and can communicate what they need to the art consultant.

Minuses

We have found when the architect or architect's team is managing the entire project, they are sometimes stretched thin. They may not always have the time to give adequate consideration to an artist longlist provided by the art consultant, limiting what is possible for the art project. Also, if the client is paying a considerable fee to the architect, the fees that then go to the art consultant and the artist can get watered down.

Architect as Art Consultant

In other cases, we've noticed that some architects will not employ an art consultant at all. Instead, they take on the role themselves. While many architects have an affinity for art, if they are busy managing projects and designing our cities, they are less likely to be plugged into the art scene the way an art consultant is. They rarely have time to build a stable of new and diverse artists. This can lead to them working almost solely with established artists or using the same artists again and again, when they should be offering their clients a variety of choices that includes diverse and new artists who will create new artworks that can appeal to new audiences.

I admit this is a personal bugbear of mine. I believe that if an organisation awards a project to an architect, then it is vital for the architect to employ an art consultant or curator who has direct links to a wide range of artists. This will ensure that the art project for the site will be managed in the right way.

Architect as the Artist

Occasionally, we have even seen some architects play the role of artist on a project. Unless the architect also identifies as an artist and has an established art practice, I would advise you to stay away from an architect who merges these disciplines. It is not best practice. The whole point of engaging an artist on a site is to have something tailored to the site that responds to the art project's narrative, and to support the wider creative community overall.

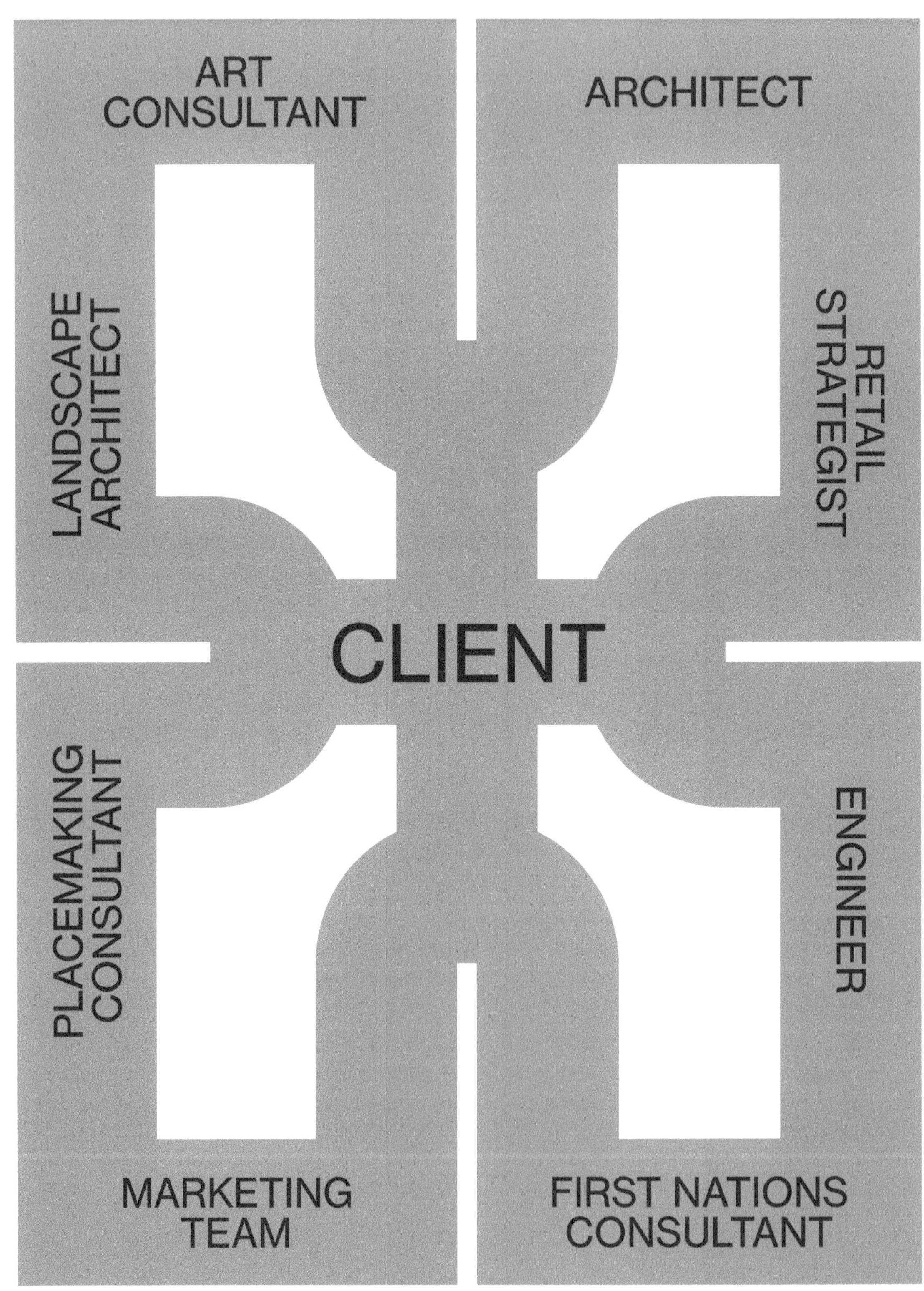
ART
CONSULTANT
ARCHITECT
LANDSCAPE
ARCHITECT
RETAIL
STRATEGIST
CLIENT
PLACEMAKING
CONSULTANT
ENGINEER
MARKETING
TEAM
FIRST NATIONS
CONSULTANT

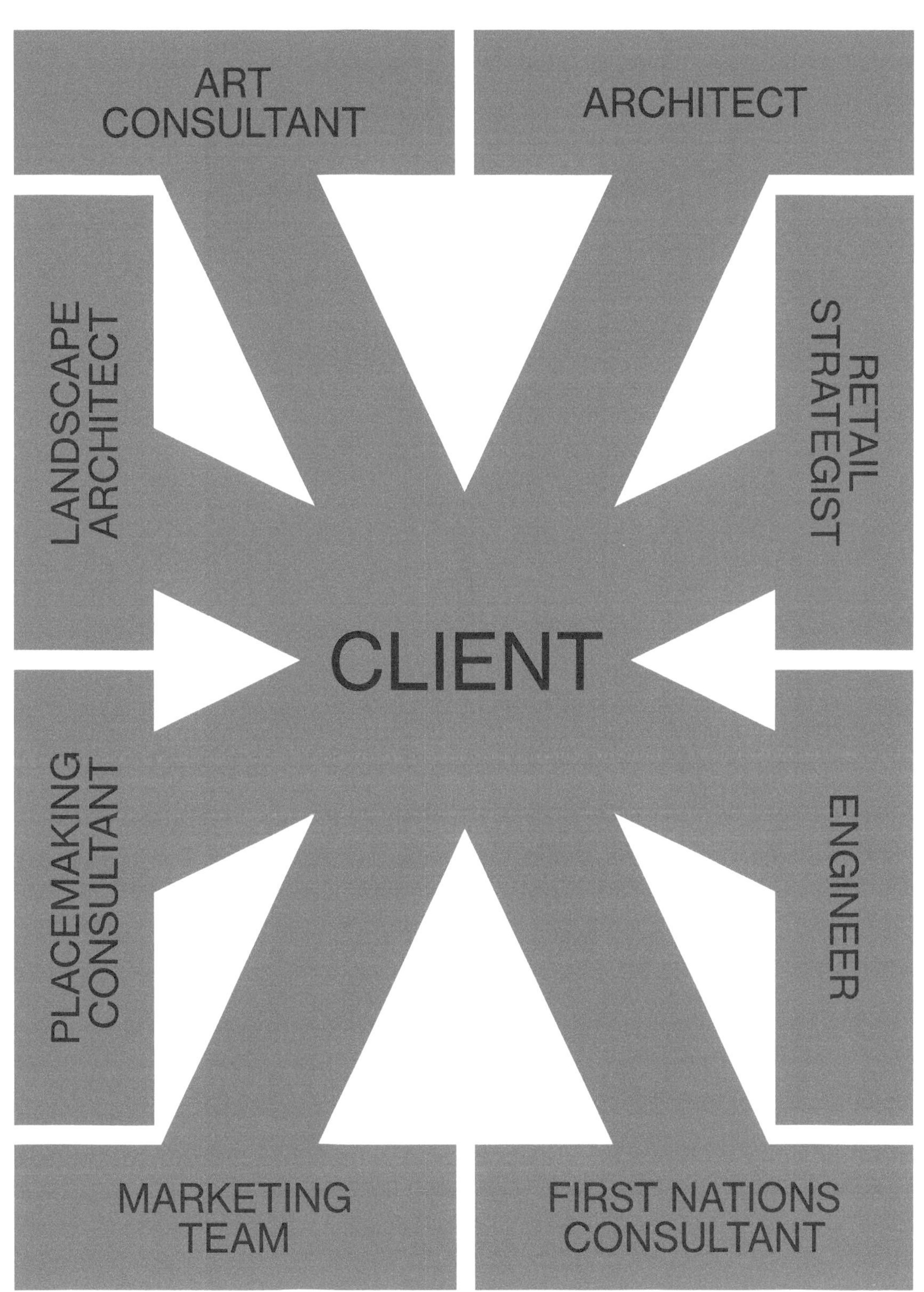
ART
CONSULTANT
ARCHITECT
LANDSCAPE
ARCHITECT
RETAIL
STRATEGIST
CLIENT
PLACEMAKING
CONSULTANT
ENGINEER
MARKETING
TEAM
FIRST NATIONS
CONSULTANT

GOLDEN POINTS

01 If your site is being managed by an architect, they will be responsible for the art on the project. If this is the case, ensure that they employ an art consultant.

02 If your architect gives you a longlist of artists to choose from, examine why they have suggested the options. Are they offering a diverse selection or the same artists they have used before?

03 Where possible, employ an art consultant directly rather than having the architect do so. This provides you with more autonomy in the art project.

THE ART COMMITTEE

On larger projects, a single art project manager, whether they be from your in-house team or an external art consultant, may need additional support. That extra support comes in the form of an art committee, sometimes known as an 'art panel', that will be comprised of stakeholders in the project.

People do get a little worried when we mention this, although I tend to use the term 'committee' quite loosely. It is true that committees can be the bane of many people's professional lives. However, a good art committee can be incredibly useful, especially if it functions as an extension of the art project manager.

As with any committee, an art committee or panel should:
— limit the membership to key stakeholder groups
— understand their purpose
— set out a clear agenda
— keep to making key decisions only
— take and keep notes for each meeting
— always provide a date for when feedback can be expected
— provide cut-off dates for when specific answers are expected.

The idea behind an art committee is for the art project manager to be able to consult with a few key stakeholders along the project's journey, for them to let others know the details of the project and its progress, and to have access to people who can support or sign off on the artwork and make important decisions.

In addition, your art committee can help to steer the project consistently and make sure that everyone's interests are represented along key points of the project's timeline. This way, each relevant department will be aware of what other possible supplementary projects they might need to commission, or other consultants they might need to employ, for you to get the best out of the money and time you are spending on your art project.

You might pick your committee members based on their position, their ability to influence and set the tone, on their knowledge of and fluency with art, or their ability to represent a key group's interests.

The rationale behind how you build your art committee will be different in every situation. If you see the potential for more art projects in the future, then consider this as well.

By maintaining a committee that can work across several art projects over time, you can also build a fluency in that committee which will bring vibrancy to your art projects and push boundaries in any future art ventures your organisation might undertake.

Like any functional committee, an art committee often brings together people or groups that have very different agendas and concerns. Following are a few possible committee scenarios.

The Corporate Committee

A corporate committee could be made up of the organisation's Client Services Manager, the CEO or the CEO's assistant, someone from internal communications or marketing, and the People and Culture Manager.

The Property Developer's Committee

A property developer's committee may be comprised of the Development or Assistant Development Manager, the Community Engagement Manager, someone from marketing, the building's owner or co-owner and a tenant of the building.

The Hotel Committee

A committee for a project in a hotel could include one of the investors in the overall project, the property owner, the hotel's brand representative, someone from the hotel's interior design team and the architect.

The Public Art Committee

For public art projects, we have often found that the art committee is likely to be made up of the Development Manager, a council member (if required for the project), a member of the marketing team and the architect.

If you or your internal art project manager identify a low level of art confidence or strongly differing attitudes in the committee, I recommend you engage an art consultant to help you and your art project manager navigate these differences. Art consultants are specialists in this area and can use their expertise to help your group find common ground, re-jig the brief, if necessary, give feedback and evaluate concepts. This will push the project further and provide helpful information to the artist. Without someone in the committee who has a good level of art confidence, you run the risk of the resulting artwork being bland or safe – an outcome that no one, including the artist, will be happy with.

Since art is so subjective, it is important that art committees be carefully guided in terms of what they are evaluating their decisions against. Generally, they are not being asked to evaluate whether they like an artwork design concept. If this is done, then you may encounter subjective responses such as, 'I wouldn't have this in my house!' or 'I don't like the colour'. This type of response is not the role of the committee. Instead, their task is to make decisions against key documents, including the art narrative for the project and the artist's brief, both of which need to be agreed upon early in the life of the project.

It is also useful to have someone, whether that be your art project manager or your art consultant, to mediate and guide feedback from the committee and how it is relayed to the artist. If the committee is not getting what it expects from the artist, they need to evaluate their concerns against what has been communicated to the artist by the art project manager. At this stage, it might be time for the art project manager and the committee to review the project's stated outcomes, brief and narrative, and decide what feedback would be most helpful for the artist to get the project back on track.

Finally, keep your art committee as small as possible. I recommend there be between four and six people in total – four is best, where possible. With more than six people involved, the decision-making and reviewing process can become laborious and end up being a chore for all involved.

Remember to keep decision points to a minimum; the more opportunity the committee has to give feedback, the more likely a random spanner-in-the-works opinion can throw off your progress.

DIFFERENT ART
COMMITTEE SCENARIOS

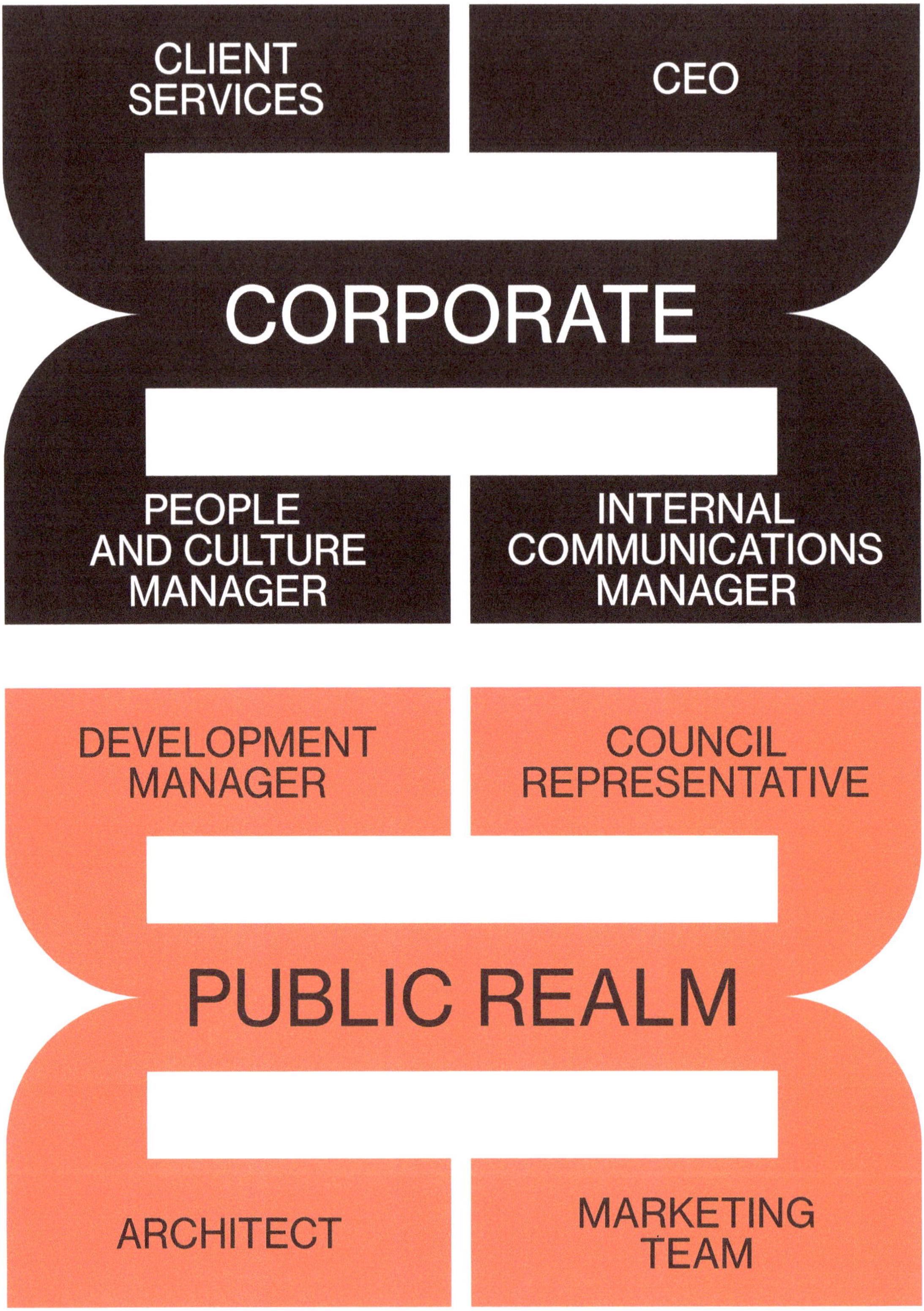

CLIENT
SERVICES

CEO

CORPORATE

PEOPLE
AND CULTURE
MANAGER

INTERNAL
COMMUNICATIONS
MANAGER

DEVELOPMENT
MANAGER

COUNCIL
REPRESENTATIVE

PUBLIC REALM

ARCHITECT

MARKETING
TEAM

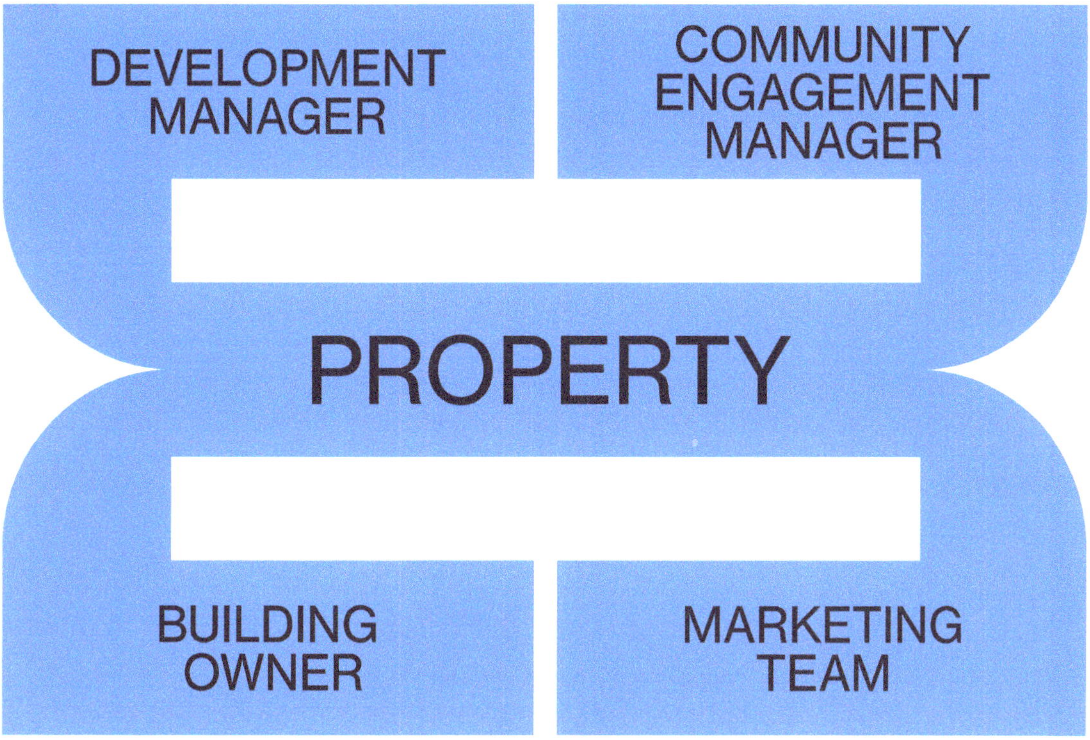

DEVELOPMENT MANAGER
COMMUNITY ENGAGEMENT MANAGER
PROPERTY
BUILDING OWNER
MARKETING TEAM
INVESTOR 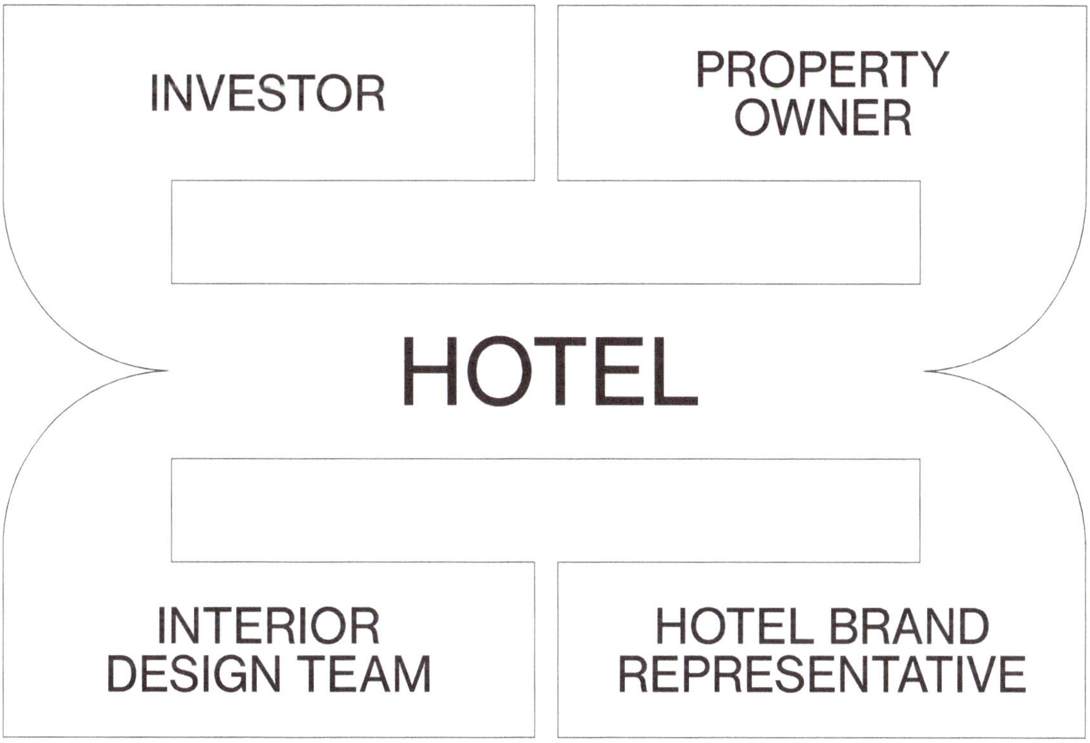
PROPERTY OWNER
HOTEL
INTERIOR DESIGN TEAM
HOTEL BRAND REPRESENTATIVE

Responsibilities of the Art Committee

For your art project, the art committee should assist the art manager in making decisions on the following stages:

- approval of the art narrative and the artist's brief
- selection of the artist from a proffered longlist, ensuring the artist chosen meets the key criteria and objectives of the development
- review of the first round of design concepts
- review of the final design concept
- the sign off on a detailed illustration and/or outline of the proposed artwork.

It is also worth noting that putting an art committee or art panel together can help manage any tricky egos or 'squeaky wheels' in your organisation, or in the greater project overall. A committee can be a great opportunity to make people feel included: as art is often a very prominent feature of a greater project, decisions made by the art committee will make a visible impact on the very public end result. Being responsible for productive decisions can be a balm to those in the committee, especially if they experience competing inter-departmental priorities. The art committee can be a really lovely way of getting a team of sometimes disparate people working well together to produce tangible results that the broader organisation will see and acknowledge.

A word of caution: even though committees can unite different interests and voices in a common process, beware of circulating committee documents widely – particularly documents that do not demonstrate the whole context of your art project. We were recently reminded of this when a large project we worked on was momentarily derailed after a committee meeting document was accidentally circulated without context to a large group of people who were unfamiliar with the project's aims. This produced negative and unproductive feedback on the artwork and resulted in it being removed from consideration even though it met the conditions of the project. An awkward exchange with the artist ensued, and time and money were wasted.

In contrast, an example of the power of a good art committee can be seen in a project Art Pharmacy completed for Mirvac's Broadway Sydney shopping centre. This project succeeded in part due to the art committee being supportive of the project throughout.

In the early stages of the project, three concepts were produced by local artist Victoria Garcia and approved by the art committee. All three concepts were signed off internally with all the committee members, so the entire committee was confident they would be happy with whichever concept would eventually be selected.

     THE PROJECT TEAM

To determine the final selection, we installed an activation in the forecourt of the shopping centre that included vinyl display decals on the ground and videos showing the three concepts. The public were then asked to vote on their favourite concept using an iPad-based voting system. The activation ran for two weeks, with thousands of votes being cast over that time. This process was the ideal way to engage the centre's customers, which included the local community, and it was a win-win situation for the artist, client and art committee.

The design concept that received the most votes by the public won, and because all the concepts were approved by the committee early on, the chosen artwork went straight into production. Once done, it was installed at Mirvac's Broadway Sydney shopping centre.

This was a great outcome for all involved, including the local customers and the tenants who enjoyed having their say on the artwork. This project is the perfect example of how an art committee can work towards a common goal and include the local community in the art-project process.

At Art Pharmacy, we also use a similar process for some of our corporate clients. In one example, we did this for a company looking to add to their art collection. We put together a selection of artworks and presented them to the client's art committee. The committee then selected three artworks which were presented to the whole company in their bi-yearly update. All 2500 employees were asked to choose their favourite, and the artwork that received the most votes became part of the company's corporate collection. This inclusive process successfully engaged everyone in the company, and all employees felt they had a say on what artwork was selected for their organisation.

The process of asking your audience to select an artwork will engage them and help them to feel like they are a part of the art selection journey.

GOLDEN POINTS

01 Keep your art committee small
and mighty – ideally four people.

02 A good art committee will
function as an extension
of the art project manager.

03 A committee is a good opportunity
for different people involved in the
greater project to have their say.

      THE PROJECT TEAM

YOU NEED TO BE ABLE TO EXPLAIN THE PURPOSE

THE BEGINNING OF A PROJECT

You need to be able to explain the purpose – the 'why' of the project.

THE BIG QUESTION

Moving forward with an art project without understanding what you want it to communicate or what a successful outcome looks like, is akin to throwing a dart into the air without a target in mind. Before you start engaging artists, you need to be able to articulate how they can succeed in their role from your perspective. For this to happen, **you need to be able to explain the purpose – the 'why' of the project** – and give them an idea of how you want the public to interact with the work.

To help you in this, I suggest you view Simon Sinek's 2009 TEDx talk, *Start with Why: How great leaders inspire action,*[3] or read his book of the same name.[4] Sinek looks at the importance of your why and how knowing this can steer your project on the right course.

Knowing your why will resolve many hidden problems from the start. It will help inform what kind of art and what kinds of artists you will bring into the project.

To successfully articulate what you want the reasoning behind – and eventual outcome of – the art project to be, start by looking at your organisation. With your art project, have you considered your organisation's mission statement and values? If not, engage with your co-workers in various departments to find out what your organisation is passionate about. Is your organisation's board pursuing a new mission with this art project? If so, identify what this is and look at how you can work towards it with the art project.

If you need further inspiration, find out if your organisation supports a foundation or charity that aligns with your principles; perhaps something there could inspire your why. Small ideas can turn into big ideas, so take time to think about your why with the people directly involved in the project, and others in the broader organisation.

Having a brainstorming session at this point can be useful. This involves gathering a few key people in a room, with a white board and someone who's willing to take notes. During this kind of session, I encourage you to ask the following questions. The resulting information will clarify and support the purpose and why of your project and provide you with a strong understanding of the outcomes you are looking to achieve.

3   Sinek, Simon, 2009, *Start with Why: How great leaders inspire action,* TEDx talk, www.youtube.com/watch?v=u4ZoJKF_VuA
4   Sinek, Simon, 2009, *Start with Why: How great leaders inspire everyone to take action,* Portfolio, Penguin Group USA.

- What are the short, medium and long-term strategies and goals of your organisation? List these goals in order of priority. (Keep in mind that one piece of art is unlikely to be the silver bullet for all your goals and challenges.)
- What are the desired outcomes of these strategies?
- Can the art project support them?
- Who will be the audience that engages with the artwork on a daily basis? What is this audience's demographic?
- What do you want them to feel or do through experiencing the artwork?
- Is there a behaviour in your audience that you want to change or encourage?
- What is the endgame of the project? For example, are you looking to engage with your local community, celebrate a cause or highlight an idea such as sustainability? Or are you looking to change the perception of your brand or gain a longer and better-quality mailing list?
- How will the success of the project be measured?

Often, the why of an art project is born out of government strategies that are adapted into an organisation's values and mission. As a result, commissioning an art project is a highly visible and engaging way for an organisation to walk the walk and talk the talk.

CURRENT IMPERATIVES IN THE INDUSTRY

In recent years, government and council policies, here and internationally, have impacted the way we see art in the public realm. Art is now mandated on new developments and these may require it to address new aims, including health and wellbeing, sustainability, the empowerment of women, or the acknowledgement, inclusion and support of the site's local First Nations communities. Keep in mind, though, that these are all specialist knowledge areas, meaning you may require specialists to help you unpack how they can be included in your project in a considerate and respectful way.

Thinking about important aims when looking at your project can inspire you to investigate the reasoning behind your art narrative, help you create a story that is authentic to the site and fully answer your why.

I'll say it again: it is critical for you and your art project manager to **understand the why of the art project.** It will help you resolve any issues that may arise throughout the project and support successful outcomes.

Wellbeing

Wellbeing is a huge trend in developments and asset management, and addressing this could be a key component of the why of your project. Wellbeing is not just about yoga and meditation or having a few extra plants around the office. I believe that in an art project context, it is also about engaging people within the site's community holistically by inspiring their imagination, sense of wonder, emotions and creativity.

Look at art therapy: research has shown that by using our hands to create something, it can be a way of reconnecting to our inner selves and increasing wellbeing.[5] In a wider context, I can think of few better ways for the broader public to reconnect with their emotions and creativity than through public art. I have seen a lone piece of artwork on an easel next to a lift in a cavernous, double-height marble lobby achieve this. While the success of an artwork in this respect is not something easily measured, consider how you can reframe the why of your project to increase its wellbeing outcomes. Think also about how the success of these can be measured; having that information could help you in your next project.

I have a seen a big shift within organisations in how they promote their employees' wellbeing. The workplace environment is now often styled to meet the expectations of staff; interior design firms are hired to 'dress' the environment with designer rugs, bespoke curtains, plants and café-style breakout areas. This shows staff that the organisation is willing to do its best to satisfy their needs by creating a comfortable environment that they can feel at home in.

Companies that pay attention to details to create a warm and inviting working environment are more likely to have satisfied employees who are proud of and appreciate their workplace. This sends a message to them about their company's values and mission. There is no reason why this careful consideration can't be extended to the art placed in corporate or public spaces, especially when many companies are encouraging their staff to return to the office. In this situation, I believe art can be used as a drawcard. If a picture is worth a thousand words, why not use art to tell your employees that you care?

5   Creativity and Recovery: the mental health benefits of art therapy, 2018, www.rtor.org/2018/07/10/benefits-of-art-therapy

Sustainability

'Sustainability' is a blanket term used on many a project brief, but I encourage you to delve deeper into addressing this issue with your art project. Art can help people become conscious of the state of our planet and assist people in negotiating the values that will support sustainable living. Any art project has the potential to convey a message that can help its audience engage authentically with environmental issues.

It is wonderful to see that there is an increased awareness about sustainability these days, although I personally feel that this awareness is about ten years too late and we still have a long way to go. Climate rallies are happening in capital cities all over Australia and all over the world. The young Swedish climate activistic Greta Thunberg has often been on the news; as a campaigner for environmental issues, she is the next generation's voice on climate change.

I'd like to think most people are aware that sustainability is a concern, and that they understand why this is the case. When it comes to art, I have seen a growing appetite for sustainable art projects that seek to change audience behaviours or contribute to solutions for environmental chaos and disruption. These are worthwhile outcomes to pursue, so think about how your project can incorporate these effectively.

Sustainable Art

In 2015, the United Nations developed 17 Sustainable Development Goals as part of its agenda to transform our world by 2030.[6] The broad aim of these goals was to help the world become a more environmentally friendly, peaceful and prosperous place. At Art Pharmacy, we endorse the UN's intentions and encourage artists to consider their role in increasing the sustainability of our planet.

In the context of art projects for large developments or public places, I would love to see more artwork that utilises materials from the project's site. Unfortunately, many organisations find that making the site's materials available to artists can be a difficult undertaking. Often when the previous structures on the site are demolished, the materials are taken straight to landfill; little thought is given to how they can be reused in an artwork. This is a shame because these materials could be used to create the most fabulous artworks that send a message to the organisation's audience around their support for sustainability.

6   Transforming our world: the 2030 Agenda for Sustainable Development, 2015, sdgs.un.org/2030agenda

A great example of this is artist Chris Fox's *Interloop* at Sydney's revitalised Wynyard Station. Chris was able to use the old station's historic 1930s OTIS timber escalators, much-loved by commuters, to create a stunning sculpture that now hangs above the new escalators at the station's York Street entrance. His work incorporates the site's past and honours its heritage at the same time as speaking of its future.[7]

A wonderful art activation project Art Pharmacy worked on that used recycled materials was *Rooster* by artist Elyssa Sykes-Smith. This was made to coincide with 2017's Lunar New Year and designed to celebrate the Year of the Rooster. It was placed in Broadway Sydney, a busy shopping centre which sees thousands of people passing through it each day. In her work, Elyssa utilised disused floorboards which she painted onsite while engaging with local shoppers.

As part of the event, Art Pharmacy set up an area near the installation where kids could also paint pieces of reclaimed wood. Elyssa then used the children's pieces in the construction of *Rooster*. So, as well as meeting the sustainability goal of the project, the activation realised outcomes of community collaboration and inclusion while celebrating Lunar New Year.[8]

Sustainable art can be created in many ways using many different materials. It could involve anything from using old plastic toys (check out the art practice of Freya Jobbins), tyres, cans or scraps of cloth to having a general focus on sustainability or ecology (ecological artist Aviva Rahmani is a good example of this).

There are fabulous artists all around the world that specialise in using recycled materials in their art. These creatives turn trash into treasure and produce work that is exhibited and seen by hundreds or even thousands of viewers. Californian artist Marina DeBris, who uses trash washed up on beaches to make her art, is one internationally renowned example. More locally, Blue Mountains' artists Kevina-Jo Smith and Jane Gillings use found objects that would normally go to landfill to create their art. They live and breathe sustainability and convey their concern for our environment through their art.

Goal 12 of the UN's Sustainability Development Goals seeks to 'ensure sustainable consumption and production patterns'.[9] This goal requires companies to work towards environmentally conscious practices throughout every facet of their operations.

------

7   View Chris Fox, *Interloop*, 2017,
studiochrisfox.com/projects/interloop
8   View Elyssa Sykes-Smith, *Rooster*, 2017,
www.artpharmacy.com.au/projects/chinese-new-years-retail-activation
9   Transforming our world: the 2030 Agenda for
Sustainable Development, 2015, https://sdgs.un.org/2030agenda

                    THE BEGINNING OF A PROJECT

At Art Pharmacy, we have seen that artists are also starting to re-valuate their ideas to work towards these goals. In doing so, they broadcast their sustainability message through their art and use their work to raise awareness.

Another way to consider sustainability is to think about the longevity of your artwork. Some artworks are temporary and some are designed to be permanent fixtures. If your artwork is a temporary activation, consider what will become of it when the activation is over. Can it be repurposed? Can the artwork be moved elsewhere and have another life?

Given these shifts in thinking, I encourage you, as a commissioning body, to think about the intent, execution and lifetime of your art project, and look at addressing sustainability through your project's why, art narrative and materials.

First Nations Art and Designing with Country
It is crucial for us to acknowledge Aboriginal and Torres Strait Islander culture, and the significance of Country in art. In First Nations culture, Country is more than a place; it is the core of a broader identity that guides the culture physically, emotionally, spiritually, and socially.

There is a symbiotic relationship between Country and art, which artists and curators have a responsibility to recognise.

Art projects in public spaces require artists that understand the Country they're working on, and the need to create art that preserves the environment and respects the traditions and culture of that community.

In recent years, art project briefs have had a stronger focus on supporting First Nations communities, with greater acknowledgement of First Nations peoples becoming entrenched in the structures and policies of organisations and their duties. For far too long, creative projects have seen the inclusion of First Nations artists and art as a token gesture, rather than an opportunity for a deeper and more considered collaboration that recognises the history of the country that the collaborators and art reside on. Fortunately, we're seeing this shift towards a willingness to embrace genuine engagement and consultation with First Nations communities.

To best ensure ethical collaboration with First Nations communities, art project policies should align with the Rights to Indigenous Cultural and Intellectual Property (ICIP), Safe Work policies, and relevant local guidelines, such as the City of Sydney Aboriginal and Torres Strait Islander protocols (2012).

Article 31 of the United Nations Declaration on the Rights of Indigenous Peoples[10], which Australia has endorsed, affirms that:

Indigenous peoples have the right to maintain, control, protect and develop their cultural heritage, traditional knowledge and traditional cultural expressions, as well as the manifestations of their sciences, technologies and cultures, including human and genetic resources, seeds, medicines, knowledge of the properties of fauna and flora, oral traditions, literatures, designs, sports and traditional games and visual and performing arts. They also have the right to maintain, control, protect and develop their intellectual property over such cultural heritage, traditional knowledge, and traditional cultural expressions.

It is the responsibility of art consultants and artists to recognise and enact these rights within the art practice.

As someone who is not of First Nations descent, I cannot advise the best way to share these stories about Country. This is something that should be discussed with those who understand through lived experience. However, art consultants of any ethnicity need to avoid tokenistic expressions of engagement; the notion that commissioning First Nations artists and starting conversations with relevant communities is a way to tick a box, to feign appreciation for the community. Often, corporations have used First Nations voices as a pillar for their own business promotion – a PR opportunity rather than genuine respect and acknowledgement.

Fortunately, today there is much greater recognition of the importance of First Nations art, culture and connection to Country in Australia, and this is becoming a significant facet in the realms of planning, design and architecture. However, we still have a long way to go and need to actively engage with First Nations communities and continue to platform their stories, recognise their culture and respect their traditions when designing with Country.

---

10   United Nations Declaration on the Rights of
Indigenous Peoples, www.un.org/development/desa/indigenouspeoples/
wp-content/uploads/sites/19/2018/11/UNDRIP_E_web.pdf

          THE BEGINNING OF A PROJECT

Accessibility

Accessibility relates to the ways that audiences interact with an artwork, and the ease with which they can do so. A good art project will consider the full spectrum of an artwork's audience, and plan ways to cater to every person's accessibility needs before installing the work.

As artworks are usually made with the intention of being seen by the public, those involved in the art strategy need to ensure that no one is marginalised by their ability to interact with the work.

Possible barriers that need to be considered are:

- Plaques. Does the message cater to all demographics of different backgrounds within the area?
- Pathways. Are there obstacles blocking people from accessing the work?
- Topography. Are there natural elements obstructing the artwork?
- Measurements. Is the work accessible to people of all heights, ages and mobility?
- Visual technology. Will the artwork be a safety risk for people with visual impairments or conditions such as epilepsy?

I recommend evaluating each aspect of accessibility throughout multiple stages of the art project to ensure that ease of access is provided to everyone, regardless of changes to the strategy.

ESG – Environmental, Social, Governmental Criteria

ESG refers to a set of standards and considerations to factor when deciding on a space for an art project. It is a set of evaluations to ensure that every aspect of the art process is completed ethically, researched deeply and follows the correct protocols and guidelines within the area with sustainability in mind.

Environmental evaluation considers how the artwork will pollute the area, natural resource conservation, the ecological footprint of the installation and the impact that the work will have on the people around it.

Social pillars examine the community and their traditions, how art will impact business and traffic as well as overall health, safety and community impact. This involves considering minority populations and how the work will affect or engage with them; acknowledging demographics within the space and accounting for all people so that everyone can interact with the work; and acknowledging or representing cultural diversity and heritage where needed.

Governmental criteria accounts for councils and government bodies that preside over the project space, as well as shareholder rights and risk management. Governing entities have insight into jurisdiction and parameters for art installations that we aren't privy to without working in collaboration with them. As art project managers, we seek approval from governing entities, to ensure that no part of the art project conflicts with the values and laws of the area.

By leveraging the three elements of ESG, art project managers can create a solid and sustainable framework for a project without hindering anything or anyone in the process.

Placemaking

Placemaking is a concept that has been around since the 1990s. The term was coined to describe the relationship between art and environment.

Placemaking is an integrative approach to urban planning and community establishment that stimulates local economies, leading to an increase in innovation, civic engagement and diversity. It's a practice that allows artists and art project managers into the suite of planning strategies for various spaces.

Project for Public Spaces, a cross disciplinary non-profit organisation with a passion for public spaces, considers placemaking to be:
Community-driven; visionary and focused on function before form.[11]

Placemaking shows people just how powerful their collective vision can be, helping them to reimagine everyday spaces and see greater potential within them.

For me, placemaking is the idea that you can take your 94-year-old, wheelchair-bound grandparent, as well as your newly mobile 18-month-old child to a space and feel comfortable doing so with both or either. In short, it is a space that is safe, engaging and exciting for all walks of life to enjoy.

Public Art and Play

The beauty of public art is in its divisiveness, that not every viewer will delight in it or resonate in its meaning, but that it serves a purpose to the space that it's in. However, as an art consultant, there is a responsibility to ensure that no community is marginalised by any public artwork in the area that they reside in, and that the work is either non-partisan or inclusive to all people. There is great power in public art that is developed with the intent to incite an emotional response, introspection or reflection from its audience, fostering a sense of belonging and connection between artwork and audience, and encouraging playfulness between the viewer and the work.

Public art has the potential to improve a neighbourhood, city or region, or simply inspire viewers to collectively reimagine and reinvent public spaces, which I've seen time and time again. Public art can strengthen the connection between people and the places they share, altering the public realm to maximise the value of the area. It can facilitate creative imagination and attention to the physical, social and cultural identities that define a space and community.

Art in public spaces can create a sense of play in areas that would otherwise be barren. In many ways, art is as interactive as the viewer makes it. Whether someone wants to connect with the work from a distance, get close to it, touch it (when permitted) or delve into the concept and semantics of the piece, the viewer can participate as they wish.

---

11   Project for Public Spaces, www.pps.org

It is this passive encouragement that allows for playfulness, as audiences are allowed to engage in a way that they're comfortable with, but the artwork invites that enjoyment.

As art consultants, we work alongside architects, businesses and private corporations, government agencies and urban planners to ensure that public art is accessible, appropriate and sustainable for the environment, while adding value to the landscape around it.

Consultation and Engagement: These are Different

When working with public spaces that are sentimental or important to a community, the consultation and engagement process allows for deeper understanding of community values and for open conversations around the intention and vision of the artwork, so that the people who will interact with it most will feel connected to the work.

As art consultants, it is our responsibility to make sure that all voices within the community are heard and acknowledged before starting the process of creating the work. This usually involves creating forums for open conversation to discuss the community values, concerns, queries and desires that surround the artwork. This process allows for greater comprehension about the nature of the population and recognises traditions, places and people of significance as well as issues that only locals would understand.

As art consultants, our role within this process is to first consult the relevant people that will be involved in the art project, such as artists, governments, stakeholders and businesses to discuss the parameters and vision for the work, and then create a forum for open engagement and conversation within the community to strengthen the vision of the artwork and the values that need to be accounted for. In this scenario, we often act as the intermediary between the art and the environment, making sure that all voices are heard, and the work is erected ethically and sustainably.

Biophilic Design

Biophilic design seeks to appease our inherent need to affiliate with nature in modern built environments. This design style relates to evolved human tendencies of seeking practicality and shelter within built structures, while catering to our innate need to connect with nature. Essentially, it focuses on aspects of the natural world that have contributed to the overall health, happiness and wellbeing of humans for centuries, and finds ways to integrate those natural elements in living and working environments.

When implementing biophilic design in an art project, it is important to consider whether all elements naturally make sense in that space, and

   THE BEGINNING OF A PROJECT

work together in unison. To best execute biophilic design practice within an art project, all features must exist within connected environments and integrated ecosystems. What this means is that you can't simply insert a natural element into a space that wouldn't organically belong there.

The challenge is finding ways to address natural deficiencies in modern settings, and initiating ways to bring those missing elements into the space in a way that repeats patterns of nature around the site, bringing them into the manufactured setting.

A critical element of biophilic design within an art project is understanding how to design with Country. This concept is used to connect ecosystems and urban spaces, while acknowledging and incorporating the unique histories and traditions of the site and the custodians that have lived there. Biophilia recognises deep connections to place, so it is instrumental to understand the connection between Country and First Nations owners of the land to create the ultimate practice of biophilic design.

Biophilic design seeks to appease
our inherent need to affiliate with
nature in modern built environments.

GOLDEN POINTS

01 Identify your why early on. Think about the purpose and intent of your project.

02 Considerations we recommend you take into account are First Nations culture and connection to Country, accessibility, wellbeing, sustainability and environmental responsibility, and community consultation and engagement.

THE PROJECT BRIEF – VISION AND OUTCOME

Now comes the fun part – kick-off time!

Now you know the why of the project, don't just power ahead blindly. It's important at this point to reflect on what you want to achieve. **I encourage you to think about what makes a great art project and what you want your end result to be** – think in a back-to-front manner to consider the intention and eventual outcome of your art project.

At Art Pharmacy, we always ask our clients lots of questions in the early stages of a project. I'd like you to think about some of these questions as well. Here are a few to get you started:

- What do you want to achieve with the artwork?
- Where will it be placed?
- What will its function be within that place?
- How do you see the artwork engaging the community?

On a practical level, try these questions:

- Who is the main decision-maker on the project?
- Do you need an art committee to help the art project manager with the project?
- Do you need an art consultant to assist the art project manager or the art committee?
- What is the timeline for the project?
- Will it need an art strategy?
- Will it need a development application (DA)? If so, when should it be submitted?
- What is the budget?
- Are there any artists you would like the art project manager and/or art consultant to include in their longlist?
- If the art project was started by someone else and you and your art project manager are continuing it, what stage is it at?

The answers to these questions will form the basis of the essential groundwork for your project. They will become points from which you can build your project, but they are not the only ones to keep in mind. Following are a few more for you to consider.

Communication

Communication is essential for the success of your art project. That is why it is important to involve the marketing and communications team at your organisation with the project – either in the role of art project manager or as members of the art committee. People in marketing are usually already plugged into the storytelling of the project and are well versed in fostering community engagement.

They know how to get the project to reflect what is important to their community, and they know how to communicate with your audience.

> The local community (external and internal) is incredibly important to the success of your public art project. It is essential for any art project manager to think about who the organisation will empower with the space being created, and how the art will contribute to this.

Communication is integral to this success – and this is where placemaking comes into its own.

Community and Placemaking

By 'community' I am referring to the local community – the people living in, or using, the space. More broadly, community can also refer to groups of people who have a particular characteristic, interest or attitude in common.

Community is an important part of any art project you may create or work on. The purpose of most art projects for developments is to successfully engage, stimulate and foster the greater project's community.

A project's community can be composed of many different layers. It includes the building's tenants, but also the general population in the area. It considers their demographics including age, cultural background and employment situations. On large developments, this information is usually researched by specialist teams of consultants who deal with engagement, planning and economics.

In addition to understanding the community you will be catering to, a big part of how your project will engage your community involves the concept of 'placemaking'.

So, what is placemaking? Project for Public Spaces, a cross-disciplinary non-profit organisation with a passion for public spaces based in New York, defines placemaking as:

Community-driven, visionary, function before form, adaptable, inclusive, focused on creating destinations, context-specific, dynamic, trans-disciplinary, transformative, flexible, collaborative, sociable.[12]

---

12   Project for Public Spaces, What is placemaking?
www.pps.org/article/what-is-placemaking

They also explain what good placemaking can do:

Placemaking shows people just how powerful their collective vision can be. It helps them to re-imagine everyday spaces, and to see anew the potential of parks, downtowns, waterfronts, plazas, neighbourhoods, streets, markets, campuses and public buildings.[13]

My own definition of placemaking is the creation of a space where you can take both your 94-year-old wheelchair-bound grandmother and your new-to-walking 18-month-old child and feel comfortable doing so. In short, a space that is safe, engaging and exciting for all walks of life to enjoy.

I could write a whole book just on the idea of placemaking! If you find you have as strong an interest in it as I do, there are national and global placemaking conferences you can attend. I went to one a few years ago and it was a great way to connect to others, see new trends and share ideas. I have included some suggestions on further reading in the References section at the end of this book.

Art Placement

Regardless of whether you are working on a masterplan development, a pocket park, a corporate collection or a room in your office or home, the placement of an artwork is an important consideration and something that should be planned early on in any project.

One of the roles of an artwork is to enliven the space in which it will be placed. For this to be authentic, the artwork should connect to the space in some way. The placement of an artwork should also be made with consideration for what is already in the area, and what you want that artwork to do for the space and its community. For example, what is the intention of an artwork that will go into the lobby of a building? Is it to welcome guests or to address the wellbeing of the building's tenants in some way? Or both? If your location is a park, is the role of your artwork to entice locals to visit? Or is it intended as a wayfinding marker?

A good starting point is to identify possible areas in your development where art could be placed. Ask your architect to send over the floorplans and work with your art project manager and/or art consultant and your interior designer to locate spaces where the artwork could go. Try to identify a number of places, both obvious and unusual.

Once you have identified some possible locations, it is time to get the artist involved. If you have an in-house art project manager, they need to action this. Similarly, if you are using an art consultant, I encourage you to involve them at this early stage, so that they can then involve the artist.

---

13   Ibid.

In fact, at Art Pharmacy, another of our golden rules is that **you must engage the artist from the beginning of the project, not in the middle or near the end, when energy, budget and drive might be waning.** This ensures that all involved in the art project are on the same page, and that the artist has every opportunity to respond to the space and your narrative when creating the artwork. This will result in a more integrated outcome for your art project.

Placeholders

Part of the initial stages of an art project involves defining expectations around what you will end up with – this might be a sculpture, an installation, a light work, an interactive/responsive art immersion, a mural, etc. The list of possibilities is long and exciting, but at this stage, I wouldn't recommend making a final decision on what that artwork will be. Instead, look at the placement and think about the artwork options you have available to you. And remember: public art is not about big bronze monoliths.

While I have seen the generic word 'placeholder' used as a stand-in for artwork on numerous architectural documents, it is actually a useful term. Using 'placeholder' means you don't have to find that exact artwork to fit your site right from the beginning. Instead, you could take it as an opportunity to engage your art project manager or art consultant, along with the artist, as creative problem-solvers – let them help you work towards a selection of art solutions for the various possible art locations on your site.

It is true that in our experience in the property development world, projects often need to define a public artwork in the very embryonic stages of the building process in order to satisfy various planning rules for council. If your project is like this, you might find that you have to 'promise' to deliver a large-scale, permanent art piece before you've even done any of the groundwork. This is often unavoidable and imposes a narrow focus over the art for the project, well before any thinking has been done about what the artwork should be communicating to the community. This can cause a 'mood board' approach to defining the parameters of the art project, not a strong conceptual approach that results in amazing art for the public's benefit. While I would like to see more developers keep a conceptual approach front of mind, if you encounter this, then remember the golden rule: **bring the artist in early**. They can help you make the best of a restrictive situation.

For art projects that are not commissioned to meet planning permission rules, it is usually the site that determines what kind of art solution is appropriate. This is where having placeholders comes in handy. In these cases, I recommend keeping an open mind about what you imagine in the space in the early stages. As mentioned, this is the perfect opportunity to have an artist come up with a solution for your placeholder.

I encourage you to think beyond murals and huge metal sculptures as a first solution. If the site allows and you are not restricted by planning rules, maintaining a more relaxed, looser definition of the artwork's 'type' in the very beginning will mean you are able to hold space for an artist to really elevate and push the project into a direction you hadn't considered. For example, they might suggest using digital art, light or integrated seating in the space, or something else that is different and exciting. After all, coming up with creative solutions is an artist's job!

I believe if more people have the courage to do this, there would be many more exciting art projects in our world.

Exploring your Art Options

When you are identifying possible locations on your site for your art project, keep in mind that successful art integrations might be large or fine-grained, responsive or passive, temporary or permanent, performative or musical, kinetic or responsive to weather. If you keep an open mind about both what the artwork might be and the location, many possibilities will emerge. Leasable floor area, emergency exits (where it is safe to do so) and services in different potential formats all become possible locations where art can be integrated. It's good to have lots of options at this point; you'll whittle them down later as the development progresses.

When thinking about the artwork, start with the experience you want people to have in the space, or the problem you are trying to solve.

Here are just a few to consider:
- street furniture or common-area furniture
- lighting, including daytime and/or night-time activation
- wayfinding and signage on a site, including in parks, open spaces or carparks
- asphalt used in city roadways and public infrastructure
- brick paving using patterning integrated into flooring and walls
- entrance and exit points on developments
- integrated into playground design
- in play opportunities for all ages, to encourage the whole community to engage with art.

Another helpful exercise when thinking about the possible artworks to go in your space is to list the constraints of each potential art location you have identified, as you know them. In a development scenario, you may not have much information on this in the early stages. But don't worry – it's OK if the sites change over time; you are just looking for a starting point. Remember to keep a loose approach and to keep your options open. This is much better than focusing on only one or two sites within the development.

A key tip here is to lean into constraints, restrictions and tricky sites. Challenging sites are really inspiring to artists and result in exciting outcomes. This is one of the key points I touch on in *Making Art Matter*.

More Questions to Ponder

There are many different conceptual and practical questions to consider when thinking about what sort of art you want on your site – the key questions being: what is the purpose of the art project? And what is the key message or mission of the artwork?

To gain an understanding of these two questions, think about the following:
- Do you want people to gather at your art site?
- Is the artwork designed to draw people into a space or intended to solve the problem of an awkward or inhospitable area?
- How do you want people to feel in response to the artwork? Do you want people to be surprised, stimulated, calmed or comforted by the artwork?
- Do you want people to dwell in the space at a certain time of day or year?

If your answer is yes to the last point, then the artwork may become what we call a 'pause' or 'ponder point' and be part of your site's overall spatial design.

Spatial design focuses on the flow of people between multiple areas of interior and exterior environments. It delivers value and understanding in spaces across both the private and public realm. The emphasis of this discipline is upon working with people and space, particularly looking at the notion of place – which connects with placemaking and community, as discussed earlier in this chapter.

Practical Considerations

In addition to thinking about location and what your artwork will communicate, I suggest that you and your art project manager or art consultant also start gathering practical information to share with your artist. It's useful to:
- Take measurements and dimensions; locate floorplans, elevation plans and any 3D modelling that might be available; and review colour palettes and information packs from the project's interior designer and architect.

- Photograph the possible spaces where the artwork might go, as well as the surrounding area/neighbouring buildings, and look at where the public flows. Think about where pause points could work.
- Identify constraints and restrictions. For example, is there a lift close by? Is there electricity available? What are the existing service points?
- Find a topographical map of the local area, especially of the region close to the site. This will help to inform the project's narrative and inspire the artist.

Outcome of Your Project

Remember to keep in mind the outcome you want for your project throughout these early stages.

Think about the impact you want the art to make and how you see the artwork engaging its audience and the site's community.

Also, think about the life of the artwork. Public art can be permanent or temporary, lasting several months, a few days or even just a few hours. Consider how the artwork will be maintained, how long it will remain on the site, and what it might be used for if it moves off the site. This is called the 'fat tail' of the project and will be discussed in more detail later.

At Art Pharmacy, we think great art projects and public artworks:
- are unique and memorable
- are well-maintained and have 'fat tails'
- have an effect on people – they surprise and delight, they inspire and encourage you to reflect or wonder, and they make you feel
- authentically connect with the community
- address the goals of a community or place
- are aligned with your brand
- demonstrate the legacy your organisation would like to leave
- sustainably support a creative practitioner and promote their practice.

GOLDEN POINTS

01 Remember that community and placemaking are two key factors in any art project.

02 Think about who your project impacts and how.

03 What is the goal and vision for your space?

04 Employing the concept of placemaking will ensure your space will attract a wide range of people because they'll feel safe, engaged and enjoy spending time there.

TENDERS

While I am not an expert on tendering, I feel it is important to cover this here from the perspective of an art consultant applying for tenders.

Why Put a Project Out to Tender?

If you don't have someone within your organisation who can take on the art project manager role and you find choosing an art consultant or curator too daunting, putting the job out to tender may be the solution for you. It may also be useful to do this if the project you are working on is very big – maybe a masterplan development – and you have specific requirements that an art consultant must fulfill. Putting the role out to tender in these cases will give you and your organisation greater choice when selecting the person or consultancy that is right for you.

What is a Tender?

On the Australian Tenders website, a tender is described as:

a formal offer to perform work in return for payment. Payment may be in the form of a fixed price or determined via a schedule of rates. Work may include the supply of goods or services or both. To win a tender, [the applicant] should understand the process and what the buyer expects.[14]
Tendering is a competitive bidding process that usually involves a minimum of three bidders. Tenders are often put out for projects led by councils or government bodies, and are mandatory for jobs where the budget is over a certain amount. Having the opportunity to bid for this sort of work offers a fair way for various consultants or agencies to express their interest and show their capacity to do the job.

What is Involved in a Tender?

A tender submission will include:
– A capability statement and biography of the person or team
  who will work on the project.
– An outline of previous experience and examples of budgets managed.
– Quotes and/or a fee proposal on all aspects of the job.
– A clear indication of delivery, curatorial direction
  (informed by the art narrative) and timelines for the project.

---

14   Australian Tenders,
info.australiantenders.com.au/blog/what-is-a-tender

How Organisations Can Help

Give Feedback

Giving feedback on an unsuccessful tender is a positive and courteous thing to do. All too often, the applicant is informed of losing out on a job via a short email that does not provide adequate reasons for the rejection.

Think about the Next Generation

Most creative projects commissioned by the state or federal government require a tender process. Generally, we find that larger consultancy businesses have more capability to work with tenders. This leaves the next generation of emerging curators or small art consultants excluded from these opportunities. They are often up against organisations that have been around for 20 or 30 years.

If you are part of an organisation putting a job to tender, consider inviting smaller businesses to apply along with larger ones, and offering some form of reimbursement for these smaller companies' time. No one would expect a builder who works on their own to do preparatory work for free, so why should a small art consultancy be expected to do so? I believe that by offering some form of reimbursement for the time and effort a smaller tenderer puts into an application, organisations who are willing to do this will not only encourage smaller businesses to apply, but help shake up the art industry and improve the tender process.

Identify who should Apply

To be successful in a tender application, the person writing the submission should know how to address the needs of the project. They need to be able to interpret what the organisation is looking for, to nail what is important. Having the best person to write the submission is key to the probability of winning the job.

At Art Pharmacy, we have found that some tenders for art projects do not specify that an art consultant should write the submission, although this practice is slowly changing. We have seen aspects of new tenders be copied from previous tenders, even though the jobs offered are different. Sometimes, the tender itself is very general as well. My recommendation is for organisations who put work out to tender to specifically tailor the tender to the art project aspect of the overall job and to clearly state who should make the submission. This will offer the tenderer a better chance of writing a strong application.

THE BEGINNING OF A PROJECT

GOLDEN POINTS

01 Tenders can be labour intensive and often aimed at large rather than small businesses.

02 Whether you are a council, government organisation or business, if you put something out to tender, ensure that you provide adequate feedback to the applicants. This is best practice and a sign of mutual respect.

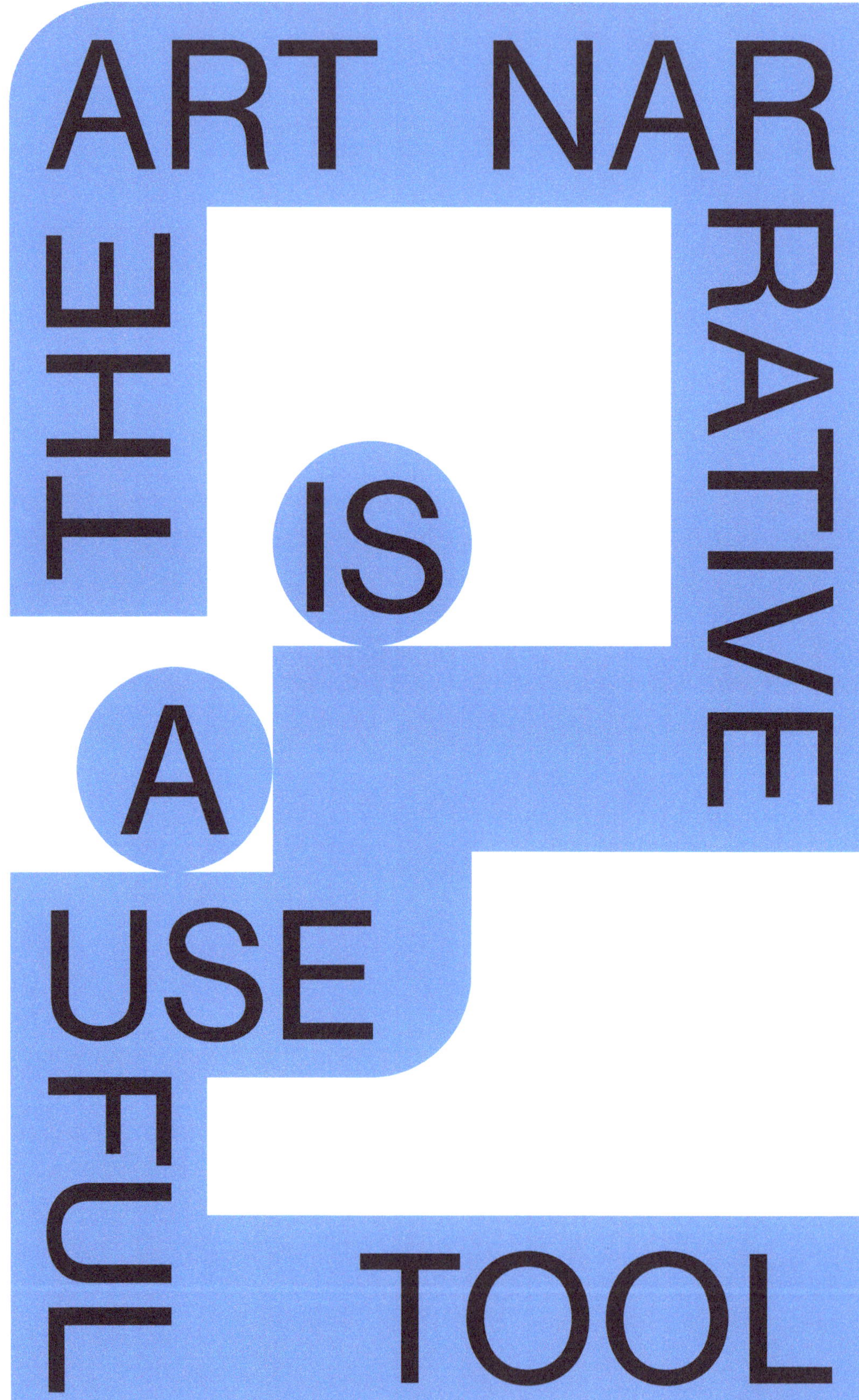
THE ART NARRATIVE IS A USEFUL TOOL

In addition to inspiring the artist/s who will work on your project, the art narrative is a useful tool.

THE ART STRATEGY AND THE DEVELOPMENT APPLICATION

These days, there are certain conditions that must be met before large new developments or development upgrades can be approved by the local council. From an art project management point of view, this involves having a clear art strategy that the commissioning body – that's you and your organisation – can include with their development application (DA).

Your art strategy functions as a checklist of what the art project will need. While you or an in-house art project manager can do this, I recommend you consider employing an external person who is familiar with this type of work. They can help you write the strategy and can take care of its ongoing management for you. This person could be an architect, a landscape architect or designer or an artist – preferably someone who is already working on the project. However, the best option would be to employ an art consultant to complete this for you, as they are experts in this field.

Regardless of who you choose to work on your art strategy, you'll need to include the following information and submit it to council, along with the rest of your DA, as part of your proposal for the art project. It is important to take time when writing the proposal – this will give you a better chance that it will be accepted. You should also clearly show that you have given considerable thought to the artwork involved in your project. Remember that for a large development, the artwork is likely to be in the public eye; no council will approve something that comes across as an afterthought.

Your art strategy will take about four to six weeks to put together. This time will cover the necessary research and development, as well as the council's time to consider your proposal. At the end of this period – once the council signs off on your strategy – you'll be ready to move on to the next stage.

After you and your art committee have chosen the artist, the project will then move through the design, construction and installation of the artwork in the site. When you are planning your art project and writing your strategy, it is important to keep in mind that the overall timing of a project can range from three to six months or longer, depending on the scale of the greater project and the type of artwork produced.

What to Include

A good starting point is to outline your objectives in a summary (perhaps one page) that clearly explains how and where your masterplan development will include artwork. Seeing this information at a glance will be very helpful to those evaluating your proposal. And remember that your art strategy will be used throughout the art project, not just in your proposal to council, so including a clear summary and information on the following areas will be useful to all who work on the project. Your art strategy will probably be between ten to 20 pages, depending on the scale of the project.

01 Overview of the Planning Context

In your proposal, think about what planning objectives the art will aim to meet. Show that you understand the current uses of the site and identify experience gaps. A detailed site analysis is essential here; at Art Pharmacy, we always make suggestions for public art in line with community, council and stakeholders' objectives, goals and current developments.

In your overview, you could also include examples of key benchmark projects, both in Australia and internationally, that are of a similar scale and nature to your project, and identify any relevant key insights and learnings from these that could be useful for your art project. In addition, aim to establish the core art and culture themes that you are considering incorporating into your art project. Give examples of a variety of artists and/or creative practitioners whose philosophies and artwork may speak to your project's narrative, and who could be provided with art opportunities by using them on the site. In short, use your art strategy to show that you have a vision for the project.

When Art Pharmacy was working on a project where we wished to give an opportunity to artists from a variety of cultural backgrounds, including First Nations and culturally and linguistically diverse (CALD) artists, we outlined how we would focus on mentorship and capability-building with both experienced and less experienced practitioners as our preferred method of artist engagement within the wider creative community.

02 The Art Narrative

One of the most important things you'll need to include in your art strategy is an outline of your project's story or narrative.

This is an explanation of the themes the artwork will explore and how they relate to the site as a whole. The art narrative for any project functions as an overlaying theme rich in meaning specific to the site. It informs the decisions that will be made on which artworks will be included in the overall project, and aids in creating a consistent place identity. A strong narrative helps the artwork to tie the precinct together.

The narrative should appropriately address and incorporate the relevant community and the site's context, and provide cues to the audience about their sense of belonging in the space. This encourages greater opportunity for community engagement and participation in the site.

At Art Pharmacy, we always provide an integrated art strategy that considers art narratives for each zone in the development's precinct, and the customer journey for each that speaks to the overall cultural narrative within the precinct.

The art narrative is an exceptionally important part of any art project.

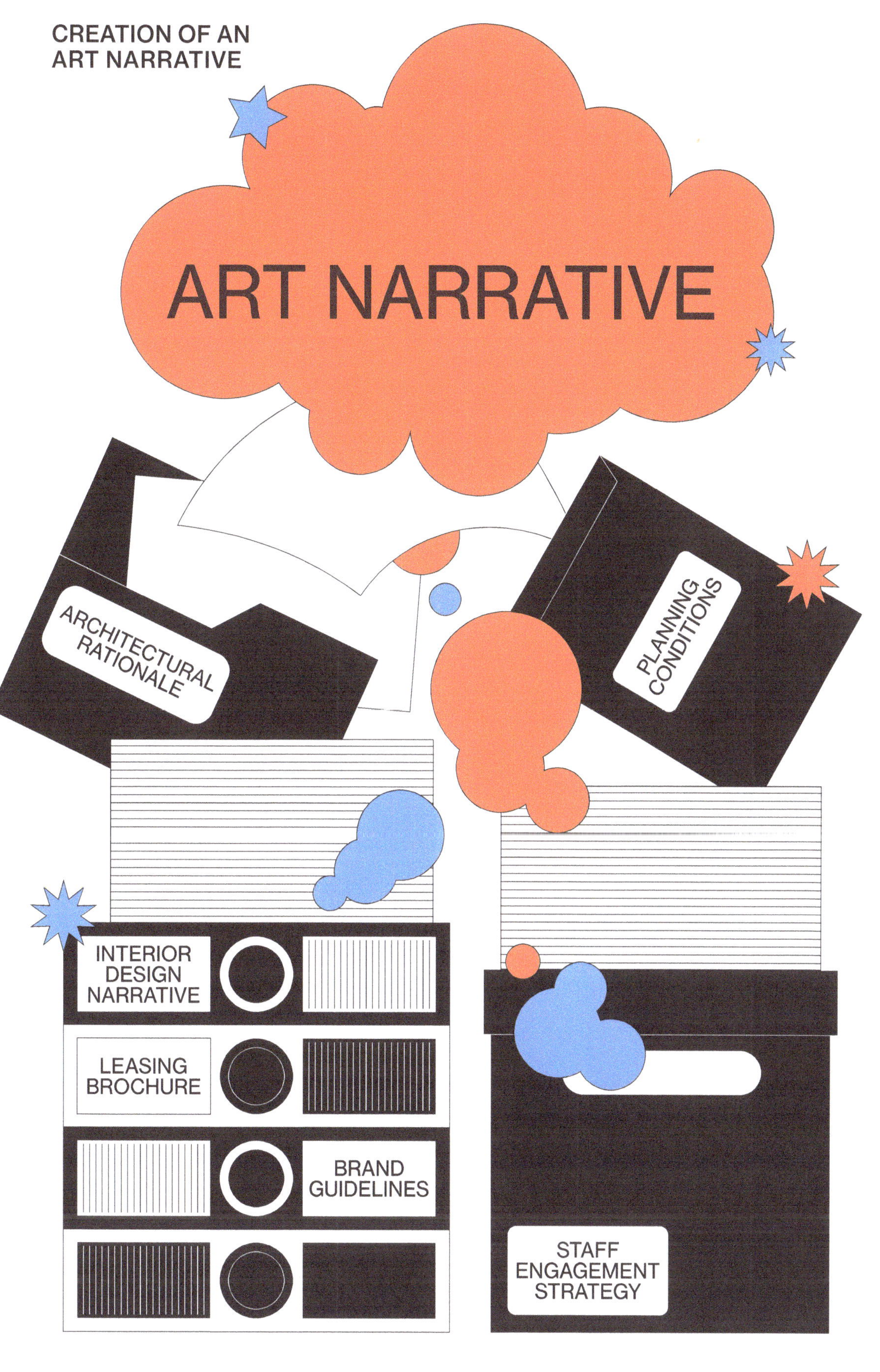
ART NARRATIVE
ARCHITECTURAL RATIONALE
PLANNING CONDITIONS
INTERIOR DESIGN NARRATIVE
LEASING BROCHURE
BRAND GUIDELINES
STAFF ENGAGEMENT STRATEGY

03 An Outline of the Vision for the Project

Visioning is a vital part of any art project and involves considering the art narrative and the placemaking principles of the site, and how these can be used to create an artwork that will appeal to diverse audiences. A strong vision for the project provides an overview of how a well-considered art strategy can act as a powerful mechanism for cultural exchange and stories, creative expression and placemaking.

04 Your Approach to Community Consultation

Community consultation is essential for understanding the values of those living in the site's area, and this knowledge will help you in your visioning process. Consultation can be carried out through surveys, workshops, information sharing and open discussion tables. It is important that in your art strategy, you show how you will reach as many of the area's cultural groups as possible to gain an understanding of the variety of points of view that encapsulates the overall vision and themes of the community. Consultation with the First Nations peoples of the area is a primary consideration and must always be undertaken as part of this process.

05 Key and Strategic Partnerships

On a large project, various partnerships will be necessary, so these should be identified early on and the nature of each examined. Be transparent about these in your art strategy, and note whether some of these relationships may need to be strengthened.

06 Public Art Options

Of course, the main reason for writing an art strategy for a DA is to show the council which artists and types of artworks you are considering for your project. To do this, you will need to provide a shortlist of appropriate artists and examples of artwork types that fit the intent of your art narrative and suit the site.

In this section of your art strategy, identify zones and activation sites. Note access points, gathering areas and dwell zones. Give examples of types of art implementations you are considering. Are they temporary or permanent? Iconic and/ or experiential? Are they designed for wayfinding or are they integrated? Perhaps the artwork might be an entry feature in the site or an integrated garden sculpture? Explain your intent as much as possible.

You'll also need to include an outline of a best-practice budget, with an indicative cost breakdown for each artwork type you are considering. Remember to ensure that the budget allows for the artist or artists to receive fair payment – that is, establish budget allocations and payment timelines for art and culture implementation.

07 Implementation and Installation

Part of your art strategy will need to outline how you plan to implement and install the artwork. This outline should include how you intend to procure the artist, how you intend to work with them to create the artwork, a rough idea of the process from concept approval to production of the work, and details of your installation procedure – including who you will be using, their credentials and examples of past projects they may have worked on. Here is also a good place to include information on the sustainability of the artwork and the maintenance it might require. I'll will be covering all of these important aspects of an art project in more detail in the coming chapters.

New Trends in Council

Dedicated art teams, some including public art officers, are now employed by most councils. This ensures that art strategies within DAs and internal public art policies are reviewed. In the past two years, there has been a big push towards all councils having a public art policy. It is now a requirement for them to have one, so if they don't already, they will be working on having one in place soon.

Recently, I have noticed that those working within councils are often creative and support the use of art within developments, like myself. While more could still be done to support those in art roles in council and within organisations, public art has become the norm rather than the exception, which is great to see.

A strong vision for the project provides an overview of how a well-considered art strategy can act as a powerful mechanism for cultural exchange and stories, creative expression and placemaking.

GOLDEN POINTS

01 Take time when writing your art
strategy to give your submission
the best chance of being accepted.

02 Your strategy should be meaningful,
authentic and strongly advisory.

03 Almost all councils have a public
art policy. Any new development now
requires the developer to submit a DA
that includes a detailed art strategy.

BUDGET, COPYRIGHT AND LICENSING

The budget for your art project is a major consideration. In some respects, determining the budget can be the hardest part of the whole venture. Sometimes I have clients who don't even want to set a budget! But, realistically speaking, if there is no budget, there is no project. You must have an overall budget for your art project, and you must also be able to provide the artist with a budget to work to when creating the artwork.

Setting a Budget

The overall cost of any public artwork is made up of many smaller costs that are incurred in the commissioning, production, installation, marketing and documentation of the art project. Aside from the artist, you'll need to employ a number of specialists to complete the job. All their fees will need to be taken into account when setting your budget.

A typical art project budget should cover the following:
- the artist's fee – aside from the creation of the artwork, this should include renumeration for the artist's initial design concepts and any amendments that might be required, progress meetings with the artist and time the artist will need to complete any relevant documentation. If you are intending to ask more than one artist to produce initial concepts (recommended), don't forget to include funds to pay for their work as well – do not expect them to provide concepts for free
- materials for the artwork, including fabrication by other technicians of specific materials if required, such as neon, other electrical components, special lighting or specific paints, etc.
- the art consultant's fee
- the fee for the writing and submission of a DA
- engineering and/or architectural renders
- legal contracts
- insurance that covers public liability and other WHS requirements
- transportation of the artwork to the site
- installation costs, which may include some or all of the following depending on the project: traffic management (if you need to close off roads for installation, for example); hire and delivery of scaffolding, a boom lift and/or a crane; council permits and engineering certificates
- lighting of the artwork (if not already allowed for in the artist's fee), including a lighting consultant's fee if you choose to use one
- travel to and from the site
- administrative and operation expenses
- copyright fees and royalties, if applicable

- plaque attribution, creation and installation
- fees for the marketing you will do to publicise the artwork, including press fees (if applicable) and the cost of a launch (if you decide to do one)
- contingency funds for unseen or unexpected costs.

Something to keep in mind when choosing an artist is that high-profile artists will be more expensive than less established or emerging artists. Depending on your project, choosing a high-profile artist may be attractive but might not necessarily represent the best value. You may find that an emerging artist is more affordable and could provide you with a fresher approach.

One thing to be aware of here, however, is that emerging artists are usually still learning how to work with property developers. You and your art project manager or art consultant may need more time to get them up to speed than you would an established artist. This extra time will need to be taken into consideration in your budget.

In addition, think about what kind of medium the artist you are considering works in, as it may influence your budget. An artist working in copper or steel, for example, will create artwork that is in a different price range from a mural artist that uses paint to cover a wall. Their fee will also be higher as the time involved in such artworks will be longer.

For some, 'budget' seems to be a dirty word, but it is vital to have a considered budget outlined before commencing an art project. However, if you really feel that creating a budget is too overwhelming, then there is the option of setting the budget as a percentage of the overall build's budget. Let's take a more detailed look at how this works.

Percent for Art

If an organisation doesn't want to set a budget for a public art commission, then the other option is to set a percentage of the build's overall budget. The risk here is that this value – usually 1% of the whole – may not always provide enough funds to produce a good outcome for your art project, particularly if your site is very large. For example, if your site is a large warehouse that is approximately 20,000m^2 and has a \$12 million refurbishment budget, your art budget would be \$120,000. While this might seem like a lot, the art this buys you is unlikely to be enough for such a large development. At Art Pharmacy, we have worked on a site like this and the budget felt quite restrictive.

On the other hand, if you have a smaller block, say around 1400m^2, and the overall budget is \$47.5 million, the budget for the art project is \$450,000. In this case, you have a much smaller site with a relatively large budget to work with.

Given this, I feel that the percentage set for art on a project should take into account the square meterage of the site and be established on a case-by-case basis. This is generally how it is done by council if they are the commissioning body.

Alternatively, you may be able to participate in a percent-for-art program if it is available to you. Western Australia's Percent for Art Scheme uses an allocation of up to 1% of the estimated total cost of public building projects to commission public artworks from West Australian artists. Public building projects with an estimated total cost in excess of $2 million are eligible for consideration in the scheme.[15]

I would love to see something like the WA Percent for Art Scheme rolled out across all states and be made a standard in private developments – with the proviso that the size of the site be taken into consideration.

Mandatory Public Art

Increasingly, public art projects are funded by property developers creating public spaces within a commercial development. Many local councils now have planning policies that require public art to be included in developments. If you need to propose an art project to meet planning requirements, your budget will be reviewed and assessed against your proposal. Budgets that do not allow for quality materials, and fair artist concept development and artist fees, will not be approved. The better the budget, the better the outcome for the whole development. For council, it is not so much the amount of money that is important, but more that the developer supports the creative community – artworks used in a development can create a greater authenticity in the project.

Occasionally, I have had a client ask me to suggest an artist they can use that will ensure the council will approve their development. But a great public art project that engages its audience is not about this – and the council knows it. The council will want to see how you are implementing your art strategy and how you are supporting the creative community in an authentic way. This will be visible through your budget – that you have allowed for thorough concept development, have a sufficient amount of money set aside and will provide a decent fee for the artist.

Creating a budget is a complex task. If you are unsure how to approach it, you may wish to bring in an art consultant who can come up with a mini strategy for you that takes your site and what you want into consideration. Art consultants are specialists in this area. Just remember to include their fee for this as a separate component to any other work they may do for you on the project, and to include that fee in your budget.

---

15   Government of Western Australia, Percent for Art Scheme, www.wa.gov.au/organisation/department-of-finance/percent-art-scheme

The Artist's Fee

There is a reason the 'starving artist' trope is such an enduring one – artists don't go home after a major commission and sit on their thrones counting money. They are very concerned with the legacy and the quality of their output. They will spend time and money to realise their unique and enduring vision for their work.

Experienced artists have learnt through trial and error how to work efficiently and turn a profit, but there is no standard for this. Learning the business side of being a professional artist has only recently been included in art courses and degrees taught in Australia, and only in some. Yet to my mind, business and entrepreneurship should be encouraged and taught alongside other art subjects, such as drawing and painting, and be integral components of all art courses delivered at college or university.

The ability for an artist to learn how to earn a decent living is something I am very passionate about. An artist's financial wellbeing depends on their facility for running their practice as a successful small business. I have often encountered artists starting out in their careers who do not know how to write an invoice or do not understand the practicalities of pricing their works. At Art Pharmacy, we are happy to play a mentorship role for these artists, but this kind of knowledge should be taught at college or university level to prepare the artist for their art career.

Any responsible art project manager, art consultant or curator should also make sure the artist is being paid an appropriate fee for their work. But what is an appropriate fee?

If you are the one setting the artist's fee, then be aware that you are commissioning a bespoke work of art for your space or for the public realm. You'll need to have a clear understanding of both the material and labour costs the artist will incur as they create the work and factor these into their fee. There are also several other ways you can support the artist financially that will ensure they can make a profit from the work they do for you.

You could, for example, provide them with an engineering certificate and any relevant architectural design documentation they may need for installation. Or, if the artwork you commission is a mural, you could ensure that the area has been cleaned and painted to the artist's specification before they arrive at the site, so that it is ready for them. If you take responsibility for these extra things, it can make a big difference to the amount the artist can keep of their fee.

I say this because in the past I have seen some artists go away with as little as 5% of their artist fee as their take-home pay. Let's look at a long-term project with a $200,000 artist fee on a large development as an example. After they have paid for materials, studio rent, transport of artwork, travel, engineering and installation, the artist may have as little as $10,000 left for a project that they have worked on for up to a year. This is not sustainable. More sustainable pay models for artists would mean more sustainable creative practices. Commissioning bodies should be aware of their role in supporting this valuable industry and budget projects and fees appropriately.

Admittedly, there is a lot of confusion about how much an artist should be paid. In Australia, the National Association for the Visual Arts (NAVA) has made great strides towards standardising rates and associated conditions for artists and creative practitioners. They cover many of the rates and situations you might come across. Paying significantly less than the NAVA rate is unethical, and you should never ask an artist to do work for free or to gain 'exposure'.

If you are not sure where to start with your artist fee, I recommend you contact NAVA and speak to a few artists (if possible) about how they charge for their work.

I believe an artist should be supported by being paid a market rate. Please remember artists have ongoing costs that include studio hire, storage, materials, couriers, marketing and more. Most importantly, you are paying for their time and talent; it takes both to come up with concepts and to create an artwork. Be respectful of this when you are deciding on the artist's fee.

A word of caution here: do not think that by including their artwork on your site you are providing an artist with a once-in-a-lifetime opportunity for exposure and therefore do not need to pay them a decent fee. This is not respectful. At Art Pharmacy, we have a minimum value proposition to ensure that artists are treated with respect. We turn away clients that don't have a realistic budget. Unfortunately, we often encounter companies with champagne tastes and a beer budget, but this simply cannot work for a public art project. You must have a decent budget – no budget, no art project.

Conversely, at the design concept stage, the artist should supply you with a detailed breakdown of the costs involved in creating the artwork. This is so you can determine whether the artist fee you have set is fair and sufficient for the artist to realistically achieve the proposed project. You may look at reviewing the budget if you don't think this objective has been achieved, or ask the artist to review the work so that they are able to take home a decent fee at the end of the day.

PROJECT COSTS

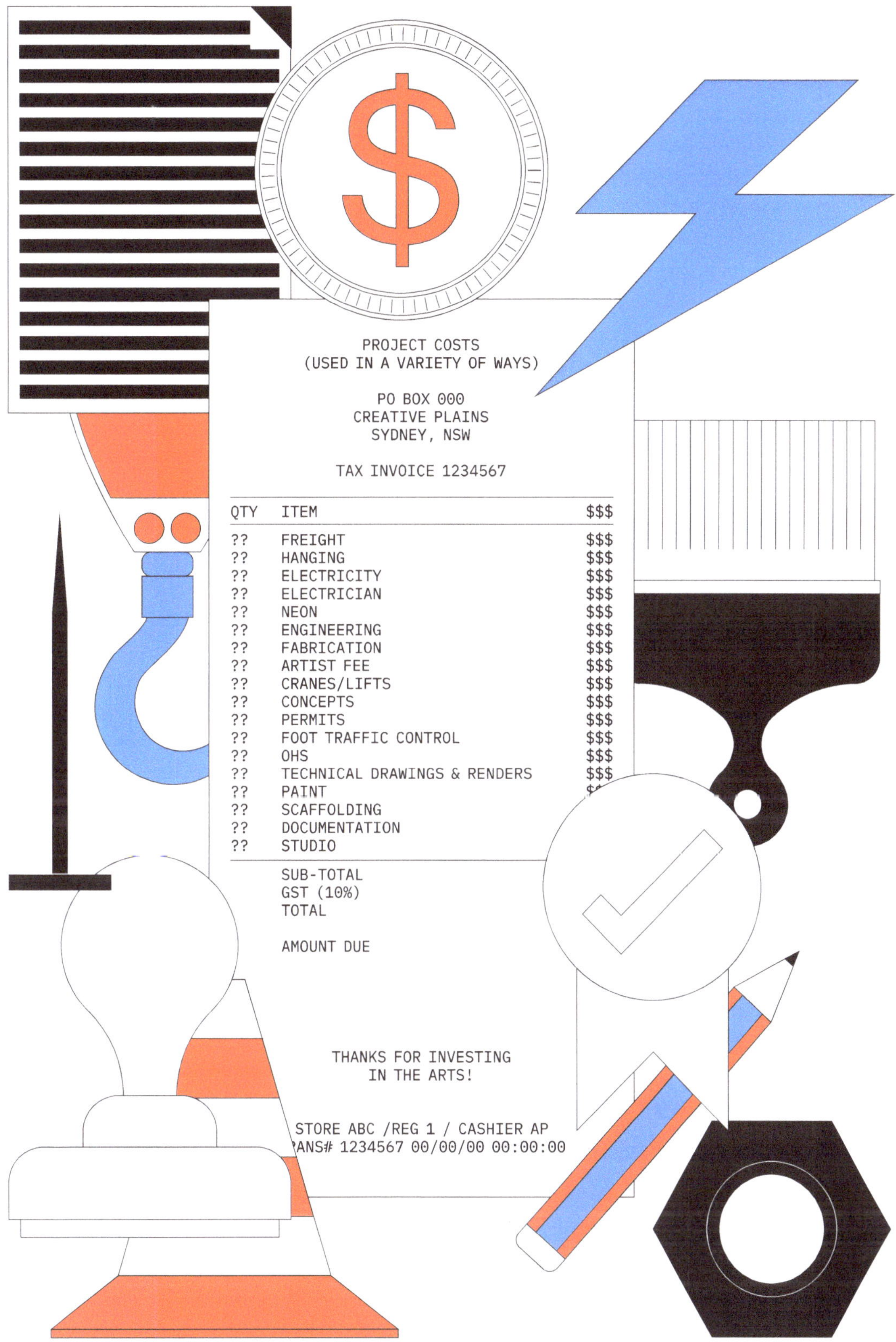

Copyright and Licensing

Something the artist's fee doesn't buy you is the copyright to the artwork. The artist will always own the copyright to their artwork unless they agree to relinquish it by selling the copyright to you. For example, if an artist creates an oil painting on canvas and sells the painting, the buyer will own the physical object. However, the artist will retain ownership of the image the painting depicts. The buyer can't reproduce the painting in any way without written permission from the artist because they do not own the copyright – the artist does.

This doesn't just apply to paintings, it applies to all artworks – sculptures, light and sound installations, and digital works. In some cases, the artist may agree to licence the artwork to you to allow you to reproduce it in certain ways and for certain purposes. If you are unsure about copyright, you can contact the Copyright Agency[16] for more information. This is an Australian site, but it also has a useful section on international affiliates.

If it is important for you to own the copyright to the work you commission, you will need to pay for this privilege and be clear from the very beginning of the project that you want the copyright assigned to you so that the artist is aware of your intentions. The transfer of copyright ownership should be detailed in the contract in a clear and transparent way with no room for misinterpretation. In many artist contracts I have reviewed, the transfer of copyright was automatically included. However, this should not be the case – the transfer of copyright is something we see as a point for a negotiation.

Similarly, if you as the client wish to license the work, you must discuss this with the artist and be clear on the terms of the license, including what royalties the artist can expect. Do this in the early stages of the project and ensure you have these terms written into the artist's contract.

<hr>

16   Copyright Agency, www.copyright.com.au

GOLDEN POINTS

01 You must have a budget
for your art project.

02 Remember that art projects are about
more than just commissioning a piece
of art – they support artists and the
local creative community.

03 Professional artists have expenses,
including studio rent, materials, insurance,
etc. Their fee needs to cover these things
and pay them for their time.

04 The artist always owns the
copyright to their work unless
they agree to sell it to you.

CREATING AN ART NARRATIVE

In previous chapters, I've emphasised the importance of your art project having a story, or an art narrative. Before commissioning any type of artwork, it is best to develop a considered art narrative that takes into account the history of the artwork's site, the surrounding area and the message you want the artwork to communicate to its audience.

Your narrative will be the key curatorial direction for the project's artwork. It really pays to embrace forward thinking with your art narrative; a lot of thought needs to be put in at the planning stage to make engaging public art installations that are relevant to place. If you do this, your project will result in an artwork that is loved and cared for by generations of people. It's this kind of core connection to the local area's heritage, values and needs that will ensure the legacy of a public art piece. If your artwork tells a good story, people will keep coming back to enjoy it time and time again, and will talk about it for years to come.

When undertaking a project with multiple stakeholders, such as a commission for a piece of public art, an art narrative is one way to help you tick all the boxes that need to be ticked (which is different to ticking boxes just for the sake if it). It can act as a guideline for the developer and the artist, and can inform the community. With a strong art narrative, you can ensure that key aspects of the site and the area around it are represented in a meaningful way. This may include addressing the heritage and geography of the site or the community and its people of significance. Or it may comment on the site's environment in other ways, such as examining the local ecology or taking inspiration from the native flora and fauna.

What is an Art Narrative?

An art narrative is the story behind an art project. It is like a mini art strategy that encapsulates your project and is sensitive to your audience – it needs to engage the imagination of your art committee, the artist you commission and the community.

An art narrative is not an artist statement or an artwork title; it's a multi-purpose statement, a cultural reference that creates a sense of consistency and storytelling within a project. It steers the direction of the art project's outcome in a refined, smooth and magical way. It is useful in many different situations – for a lobby activation in a hotel, an artwork in a common public space such as a park (where it would also cover associated community engagement activities), for guiding a private art collection or shaping a public art trail.

The idea to create an art narrative for each project came about early on when I received a very long art strategy – over 100 pages. The theme did not fit the space or the location, which was a hotel in Sydney. We decided very quickly to change the theme and give the project a more considered story, one that was authentic and meaningful to the people who would visit the hotel. This new art narrative made a world of difference to the final artwork and the project's outcome.

I really enjoy putting together an art narrative for a new project. It is a great way to start the project and works to steer it in the right direction. It's also an opportunity to bring everyone involved together and gets them in sync in a happy way.

Think locally – one of the keys to writing a great art narrative that speaks to the community is community consultation. It's the locals who will be walking past the artwork every day, so they should be getting a say in what they'll be seeing. You could do this by holding a public meeting and inviting locals to discuss the project or by gathering information through a survey.

Be authentic – write in your own voice, be clear and direct. The art narrative shouldn't be too long – between two and five pages – otherwise it can be overwhelming. Be wary of art jargon; art narratives do not need to be highbrow, complicated or elaborate.

The purpose of your art narrative is to outline the intent of the art project clearly and in a way that everyone understands. This ensures all involved in the project – including the artist, architect, interior designer and project managers – are on the same page.

A good art narrative will help guide the artist. Defining the story you want to tell will allow the artist to find commonalities and synergies that they can incorporate into the artwork for your project. The art narrative will become the glue that binds the artist, the commissioning body, the intention of the artwork and the location together.

The art narrative is not your brand motto, or a marketing or advertising document. It is a statement that is sympathetic and authentic to the development and/or your organisation's values, and a simple, fun and playful idea that stands on its own.

Your art narrative should also be endorsed and supported by your art committee. A strong narrative will assist the committee with making decisions about the project, including what kind of art will be required, what kind of artist to select, what materials might be suitable and what subject matter to explore with the work. The art narrative guides the whole project and offers a consistent overview to give to the artist to interpret and use. It will ensure a conceptual consistency throughout the project and all related activities.

A good art narrative should also be distillable into something that people can easily grasp and walk away with. This might be in the form of a phrase, poem, song lyric or character. It could be made up or refer to established cultural elements and tropes relevant to the site or the community. It might even be a question. As with the broader art narrative, whatever this might be, make it fun, engaging, local and authentic. I recommend getting out the whiteboard and playing with some ideas here – you, your art project manager and your committee could brainstorm together on this one!

If you are having trouble crystallising an idea into a strong narrative, it can be very helpful to come up with a few different options and run them by your art committee or decision-maker.

In a recent Art Pharmacy project for the Melbourne branch of a globally renowned professional services company, we were asked to put together some suggested narratives to support a corporate art collection because the company's art committee were having trouble clarifying what their art narrative should be. During a workshop with them, we identified different parts of their company philosophy that were important to the group and created three distinct narratives which we presented to the committee.

The committee quickly eliminated one of the options. It was decided that the other two options could be amalgamated to make one strong narrative that encompassed the committee's intent. We found the discussions the group had around the two remaining narratives were very productive. They helped to trim away extraneous strands in each, and the final narrative ended up using the strongest ideas from both. This narrative was then used to inform the collection.

Also, don't be scared to combine two quite different art narratives to make one strong, juicy one that has contrast and contradiction built into it – this can provide great food for thought for a group of artists and the artwork's intended audience. From an art collection curation point of view, this collaborative process can bring an engaging tension and dynamic to the collection that wouldn't exist otherwise.

In this sort of scenario, I recommend that you employ an outsider experienced in art storytelling to guide the process, such as an art consultant, creative agency or an architect who works with creative concepts. They will be able to pull all the committee's ideas together and ensure the resolution is achieved in a smooth and fair way.

The process of defining an art narrative may also be useful to your business in other ways. It's often the only time a group of an organisation's key people come together to distil a great deal of information about the project into a simple idea that can give everyone a clearly defined scope. With this in mind, when you and your art project manager and/or art consultant and art committee come together to create your art narrative, I encourage you to think about who you are, who your organisation is (and its philosophy and mission) and about the greater project as a whole. Then ask, what can this art narrative do for the company?

     THE PROJECT STEPS

Make the most of the creative thinking you and your art committee will do. Creating an art narrative is an opportunity to discuss the project in a united way and can be one of the most enjoyable and creative elements of the greater development project.

A simple, direct, digestible and authentic art narrative can condense a lot of material associated with an art project – brand documents, leasing brochures, the staff engagement strategy, marketing flyers, architectural concepts, interior design narratives, intended community engagement outcomes, the social media strategy and more – into something that the artist can address directly with their work. This way, you will have some idea of what their response might be. To give an artist a huge chunk of documentation without adequate direction risks them latching on to a concept that you don't want to emphasise.

Perhaps the best way to think of what makes an art narrative is to imagine taking all the project's many different and important requirements and pouring them through a large funnel so that the elements merge harmoniously into one distilled, clearly articulated, digestible end-concept. This end-concept is your art narrative and will guide people on how to work on the project.

While all involved should refer to the narrative, it is the artist's primary job to engage with and enhance it. The narrative should drive the artwork they create for the project. If, in the early stages you sense that you and the artist are not seeing eye to eye, it may be because you are not inclined to tell the same story, or that you need to massage it out to get a solution that suits you while not compromising the artist's vision. It may also be worth considering whether the art narrative needs to be revisited and workshopped again by you, your art project manager and/or art consultant and the art committee, perhaps in collaboration with the artist, to reach a good compromise.

The Art Narrative and the Artist

All artists understand and respond to narrative. Storytelling and social commentary are special components of what artists do; they strive to imbue meaning into their work. This meaning is based on how they see and experience the world, their culture, their hopes for the future, their relationship with the environment and other people, and much more. By employing an artist and providing them with a strong narrative you are tapping into their ability to embed rich layers of meaning into their artwork. Through this, they can reflect the message you want your art project to communicate to its audience. I encourage you to embrace this aspect of commissioning art. In doing so you will not only support a creative community, but also be rewarded by what an artist can bring to your project.

Further to this, if you are employing more than one artist on the project and will commission multiple artworks, a clear and inspiring art narrative can bring them together as a group and unite their artworks into a cohesive collection. Each artist will interpret the narrative in different and individual ways, but the resulting artwork will belong to one family, one body of work that is informed by your art narrative.

Following are a few examples of some past art narratives Art Pharmacy devised around the theme of Australia. In some of these cases, several artists were asked to respond to the same narrative, each producing their own unique interpretation.

The Modern Larrikin: Fun, humorous, engaging and quintessentially Australian. We incorporated this idea into a narrative for a large hotel group and used a sulphur-crested cockatoo to embody the modern larrikin – cheeky, loveable and funny.

Beauty and Abundance: This narrative was created around the beautiful and abundant fauna and flora of the project's local area.

The Australian Landscape: A narrative that was suggested to capture the beauty of our Australian landscape, and the varying responses it can inspire.

Contemporary Urbanism: This is a narrative that reflects the feel of city streets. It inspired artworks that interact with the street conceptually, thematically and/or aesthetically.

In addition to inspiring the artist/s who will work on your project, the art narrative is a useful tool to have during the artist selection stage, especially if you or your art consultant open the project to expressions of interest.

The artist/s should address and embrace the art narrative in their application, so seeing how they do this will help you pick which artist/s are suitable for your project.

Case Studies

Following are some case studies that demonstrate the value of having a considered and thoughtful art narrative. Although they are all very different, each one resulted in a fantastic art outcome.

Case Study: Beauty and Abundance

In 2019, Art Pharmacy took part in a community project in Windsor, NSW, where the Hawkesbury City Council engaged us to deliver place-relevant and community-centric murals to high-profile sites in Windsor Mall. Brother and sister First Nations artist team David and Noni Cragg and artist Thomas Jackson (all based in Sydney) were commissioned to adorn the mall's walls with imagery interpreting the history of Windsor's local native flora and fauna. These stunning designs were the result of a vigorous community consultation process to develop an art narrative that truly reflected the values and priorities of the community.

The Art Pharmacy team engaged with local community members in a public meeting where we discussed what the community would like to see preserved and addressed by the project. From there, we set up a mailing list to keep the community updated, collecting feedback and information along the way. We even set up a website to keep the community informed about each stage of the project, which we regularly updated to show the project's progress in real time.

The information we collected during this process helped to inform the longlist of artists we put forward to the council, including a selection of artists with connections to the local area. An art committee was formed that included a range of representatives from the local community to help with the selection process of the artists and the final design of the murals. Doing this was essential in ensuring that the community's needs and values remained at the heart of the project.

From all the information collected, Art Pharmacy was able to form a public art narrative which would ultimately become an artist brief and inform the artists' design concepts. The narrative was titled 'Beauty and Abundance' and it became the core of the artists' designs.

We learnt from the community that it was important to honour the deep and rich heritage of the area, which spanned more than forty thousand years, while also recognising the new, fresh life that filled the Hawkesbury region. In their response to the narrative, the artists were required to draw a connection between the old and the new in Windsor. The other aspects they needed to include were the rich native wildlife and the role that fresh food has played in the area. These have drawn the community together in the past and present, and will do so in the future. Ultimately, all plant and wildlife imagery included in the final murals depicted species that are native to the area.

By making sure that the community had a central role in shaping the story these murals told, our project had a unifying effect in the town, and locals felt they had some ownership over the end result.

This success has broader connotations. If the public are invested in the narrative and embrace the resulting art, they will respect the work and take care of it. Hopefully, this will see the community engage with the council to push for more public art in their area. In this case, the project's successful art narrative could be the silver bullet that encourages bigger investment into arts and culture in Windsor.

Case Study: Queensland Themes

In a contrasting example also from 2019, Art Pharmacy worked on a project with property management and development company ISPT where we installed a huge digital art activation in the lobby of their premises located in National Bank House, 100 Creek Street, Brisbane.

ISPT was after a long-term digital placemaking project for their offices that celebrated Queensland with custom-made, hyperlocal content. To ensure that the installations were visually consistent and relevant to the setting, we only used artists that were based in Brisbane. Six themes – earth, water, sand, rainforest, coral and sky – informed a high-level narrative that was place-relevant and not too prescriptive. Each artist took inspiration from a particular theme. This successful project was a year-long activation – the first of its kind in Australia – and garnered a positive response from tenants of the building and the broader local community who visited the site.

Case Study: Jason Wing's *In Between Two Worlds*

While this is not a project Art Pharmacy worked on, it is another great example of how a good art narrative can produce wonderful art that engages the community. *In Between Two Worlds* by Jason Wing (2011), located in Kimber Lane, Haymarket, Sydney, was commissioned by the City of Sydney.

When Jason was commissioned to do this work, he spent two weeks sitting in Kimber Lane observing who used the space and how. After this observation, Jason asked local shop-owners what they'd like to see in the lane, and how they'd like to see it utilised more. This information informed his design, which he describes as 'resembling another world, another place'.

An interesting play on the narrative for the project came up when safety lighting had to be installed. This was a practical consideration, but also made the alley more inviting, especially after dark. While red or yellow was the preference of elders in the community due to the association with prosperity, Jason chose blue to highlight the colours of the artwork and to help it stand out from the other lighting in the area. Jason was able to convince the elders of the community that blue would suit best as it was a colour consistent throughout earth, wind, fire and water, the elements being an important part of Chinese culture.

While the mural didn't reflect all of what the community wanted, Jason was able to resolve the issue using the narrative of the work. In his words: 'the mural didn't totally conform, but that goes back to the modern Chinese person: we're a bit different'.[17]

17   View Jason Wing, *In Between Two Worlds,* 2011, www.culturescouts.com.au/stomping-ground-blog-source/2018/5/1/ artist-jason-wing-on-weaving-culture-heritage-and-community- into-public-spaces

GOLDEN POINTS

01 Crystallise the story behind
your art project into an authentic,
simple and effective art narrative.

02 Consult with the proposed artwork's
community – in many cases, this will
be the key to making meaningful
connections between your artwork
and its audience.

03 Be open to the artist/s contributing
to the art narrative – sometimes they
can help you to make it stronger.

THE ARTIST BRIEF

Once you have finalised your art narrative and it is signed off, you are ready to move to the next stage of your art project: writing a comprehensive brief for the artist. **This artist brief will be the foundation of the artwork and will be used by the artist to create concepts that respond to your art narrative.**

A clear artist brief is vital to the success of an art project. It is the backbone of everything the artist does in relation to the artwork they produce for you. While it will aid them in all practical aspects of the artwork, it will also include the art narrative. This means it will define and manage the conceptual impact of the artwork. If you get the artist brief right, the result will be an artwork that will inspire a broad range of people. Depending on where your artwork is located, this could be your customers, colleagues, staff, the local community and/or the public.

The artist brief is not just about giving the artist a checklist of what sort of physical artwork is required and when it should be delivered. The brief must inspire the artist to use their skills in crafting an experience while communicating a story. Essentially, your artist brief is the culmination of much of the work you have carried out on the art project so far. Together with the people you have selected – whether that be your art project manager, your art consultant, your art committee, or even all three – you'll need to write the artist brief in a way that will outline the story you want your artwork to tell. Along with outlining the practical requirements of the artwork and its story, the brief will be where you set the budget and where you will define the markers you'll later use to measure the success of the project.

It is in everyone's interest to get this stage right. With a good brief, all stakeholders involved – including the artist – should be able to easily follow the progress of the project, be aware of expectations and know the details. A comprehensive brief can also be handed from manager to manager if someone new comes onto the project, and thereby helps to cover your key person risk.

The artist brief must be done before engaging an artist to work on your project. While this may sound obvious, I have seen some artists be taken on without being given any guidance of what is expected of them. Another important reason to have the artist brief ready before employing the artist is that it will be included in the artist's contract for the commission. And you should ALWAYS have a contract with an artist – to protect them and you!

As the brief will go into the artist's contract, you must make it precise and keep it updated with any changes that may happen during the project. In a contract, the devil really is in the detail.

Most project managers will have their own way of managing information on projects and briefing suppliers. However, I would like to define creative practitioners as special suppliers who need to be briefed in a particular way.

A lack of understanding about how artists work often results in hiccups during a project. If the brief is not articulated in a way that the artist can understand, or left too open to interpretation, your project may not go in the direction you intend.

Without adequate direction, the artist's perspective of a project may be very different to that of the commissioning body and its project team. That's why the artist brief should be clear and comprehensive, and written in a language that makes it easy for stakeholders and the artist to understand.

A wishy-washy engagement with an artist that is low on detail can leave things too open to interpretation and lead to miscommunication. It might result in an outcome that doesn't meet your expectations, leaving both you and the artist unhappy with the end result. Professional relationships can break down and this can deter you and your organisation from working with that artist again, or doing more art projects in the future. A well-considered (but not rigid) brief prevents this from happening and maintains amicable professional relationships.

On the flip side, some artists might find that a clear and detailed outline of expectations intrudes too much on their artistic freedom. Depending on what you want from your art project, if you encounter this, then perhaps they are not the right artist for you. In a corporate setting, particularly if you have a specific outcome for your art project in mind, I believe the best solution is to select an artist for your project who understands the value of a rigorous project structure and who is able to offer clear deliverables.

If you are employing an art consultant on your project, then they will write the artist brief and manage the whole process for you – or help your art project manager do this – including keeping track of the artist's progress. And a good art consultant will keep all stakeholders' interests in mind – yours (the client), your team's and the artist's.

What Should be Included?

The artist brief should be written clearly and concisely, and must cover all the key information about the project with specific details added where required. It should include:

- the name of the client and what the organisation does
- the location of the site
- the art narrative (signed off by the art committee)
- background information on the site and the local area, including any heritage information (if applicable)
- detailed plans of the site and the development, including a topography map, all floorplans and accessibility details, as well as any information on any physical constraints the site may have

- concept direction – guidance for the design concepts the artist will create for you to choose from
- a timeline of the project that pinpoints key progress dates, including dates of delivery and installation
- information on installation
- a budget for the artwork.

While some of the above points will call for different levels of detail (I'll go over that shortly), what I wouldn't include is extraneous information that may only be relevant to the greater development project. This can lead to the artist becoming overwhelmed. The brief should only have key information that is relevant to the artwork and outcomes of your art project.

In the early stages of your art project, especially if you have not yet selected the artist for the job, the artist brief may start out being low on detail. However, by the time you are ready to engage the artist, and particularly before you put their contract together, the rest of the required details should be refined and added into the brief.

In addition to providing them with a brief, we recommend giving the artist an opportunity to visit the site early on, preferably with the art project manager or art consultant, even if the site hasn't been worked on yet. Simply going for a walk around the site – even if it is just a stroll around the block of the proposed area – will give the artist a spatial understanding of where the artwork could be placed, and will offer them some context for the details in the artist brief.

Now that we have established the importance of the artist's brief, let's take a closer look at the information that needs to be covered.

The Client

It is important to provide some information about your organisation and what it does so that the artist can understand your organisation's business and values. At this point in the project, you don't need to include names here, as either you, your art project manager or your art consultant will be the primary contact for the artist. This will avoid confusion and the risk of other people providing conflicting information.

Location

Include the address and the name of the building or site.
It is also useful to detail the demographic of the area
– that is, who the main audience for the artwork will be.

On a deeper level, include information on where you are
thinking of having the artwork within the site (and if you aren't
sure, remember that the artist can help you with this). If you
have an idea of how you'd like the artwork viewed – perhaps
it might function as a pause point within an office space, area
or precinct, or be intended as a meeting point – include notes
on that as well. This is all good information for the artist
to have early on.

Background and Historical Context

Only include further background information if it is relevant
to your art project's narrative and outcomes. If the artwork
must incorporate heritage interpretation as part of your site's
planning permissions, provide the artist with the relevant
historical research.

Some artists will go deeply into the background and history
of the location as part of their practice so may appreciate this
sort of information, or they may prefer to do their own research.
Others don't like to be clouded too much by history.

Just remember to include this information only if it is relevant
to the planning of the project or if it is an integral part of your
art narrative, otherwise it could overwhelm the artist. The artist
can, and will, ask for more information if they need it.

Narrative

You must include the art narrative for the project – it will be
the inspiration the artist will use when designing concepts
for the artwork.

Site Details and Site Restrictions

Here is where your brief needs to include details that will
help the artist consider how the artwork will work in the space,
including how the physical dimensions and restrictions of the
area will impact on the artwork, and how they can address
what you want for the space.

A good brief should include the following:
– photographs and detailed drawings of the site showing what
  the site is. For example, it might be an internal or external wall,
  a public space, a digital art screen, etc.
– photographs and detailed drawings of the constraints of the site
  illustrating where the artwork needs to fit
– detailed measurements of the area where the artwork is intended
  to be situated
– if the site is external, relevant details of the surrounding area that
  may impact the artwork or installation of the artwork. For example,
  is there a big tree on or near the site that might shade the area?
  Is the site near a busy main road? Is there a bus stop nearby that
  people use or are there lots of pedestrians who walk by the site?
– an indication of the location of the artwork. For example, if the
  artwork will be inside a building or space, where will it be located?
  On the ground floor or on a different level of the building?
  Which level will allow access to the artwork?
– if the site is internal, detailed height and width restrictions so
  that the artist will know how big a 'canvas' they'll have to work with
– information on lift access and the size of the entrance or delivery
  point (I have encountered occasions where an artwork couldn't be
  installed in its site because the doorways and/or lift were too small.)
– weight loadings (floor and ceiling), especially for larger sculptural works
– fire loading restrictions. That is, what materials can be used and any
  ratings the artist will need to be aware of
– how the artwork will be secured. For example, will the artwork need to
  sit on a plinth? If so, will it require museum wax? Will it sit on the floor,
  be wall mounted or hung from the ceiling?
– details on lighting and any restrictions around lighting. This is
  important if the site of the artwork is near a road or transport corridor
– confirmation of what services are available on the site. For example,
  does it have power and/or water?
– how the artwork will be protected if it rains during the installation process
– confirmation of the hours of operation of the site. For example, will
  it be open 24 hours a day during construction? When can the artist
  access the site? After installation, when will people use the site?
– information on where, when and how the artwork should be delivered
– details of loading dock access and the hours in which it can
  be accessed.

Design Concept Direction
Giving the artist direction on what sort of artwork you have
in mind will help them come up with relevant ideas, or 'design
concepts', for you to choose from. This element is a very
important part of the brief.

TIMELINE

Aside from the information that will guide the artwork, the
brief will need to include a timeline that includes any expected
progress dates for artist deliverables and the due date of the
final artwork. This timeline should be very specific – state the
key dates and feedback points, outline what you expect to be
delivered and when, and always set a date for installation
of the final artwork.

Once you have your timeline, aside from providing it to
the artist in the artist's brief, remember to give a copy of it to
anyone else directly involved in any aspect of the artwork's
progress – such as the art committee, who will be involved in
deciding which artwork concept to go with – so they can put
the project's key dates in their diaries.

I've included an example of a timeline that shows the
important milestones you will need to consider for your project.
I have based this sample on a timeline Art Pharmacy had for a
complex art project that consisted of a curated art collection.
On that project, 13 artists were involved, and the works were
a mix of site-specific commissions and existing works, so
milestones were essential to keeping everything on track.

This sample schedule takes into account that you will have
more than one artist at the beginning of your selection process,
and outlines a project with a 16-week turnaround. However,
depending on what your project involves, this timing may be
shorter or longer. A large sculpture, for example, can take
anywhere from three to six months (or longer) to manufacture.

W1 Week 1: Artist Brief Issued to the Artists

The artist brief is issued to the shortlisted artists. This will include a project timeline and a clear indication of the due date for their design concepts. Each artist will be expected to produce three initial design concepts and include information on how the proposed artworks respond to the art narrative, as well as any other relevant information about the artworks (materials, size, etc.). The artists will have approximately two weeks to work on their concepts, but this time can be up to three weeks, depending on the project.

W2 Week 2: Check in with Artists Regarding the Artist Brief; Site Visit

The art consultant or project manager will check in with the artists to see if they have any questions about the brief and to see how they are faring. This is also a good time for the art consultant or project manager to arrange a site visit for the artists so they can familiarise themselves with the location.

NOTE: If an in-person site visit is not possible, this go-through of the site's details with the artists should be done via Zoom.

W3 Week 3: Artists' Design Concepts Due

Each artist will be expected to email their initial concepts to the art consultant or art project manager by the due date.

NOTE: The art consultant or art project manager will need at least two full days to review all the concepts, perhaps longer if there are many artists submitting. This time will allow them to go back to the artists with any queries they might have before the concepts are presented to the art committee.

Week 3: Art Committee Meeting 1
– Concepts Reveal (Round 1)

Once the art consultant or art project manager has gone over all the submissions, they will present these to the art committee. I can't emphasise enough how critical this meeting is, especially if more than one artist has been asked to provide initial design concepts (recommended) and the project requires only one artwork. Ample time must be allowed in this meeting to go over each and every design concept, because it is at this point that the committee will select the artist and the design concept they want to go with.

However, some committees may need still more time to decide. If a final decision can't be made in this first meeting, the art committee must be given a clear date for delivering feedback on the options that are being considered (usually within a week or two at most). At this point, the art consultant or art project manager will need to record any comments that are made about the artists and design concepts. It is important to have this information because some of the artists in the shortlist will be rejected after the final selection is made and they should be offered some feedback as to why.

Another of our golden rules at Art Pharmacy is that **it is always best practice to give the rejected artists an idea of why they were not accepted for the job.** Likewise for the successful artist – take notes on the reaction to each of their design concepts so you can explain to them why one was chosen over the other.

NOTE: If this committee meeting can't be held in person, it should be done via Zoom.

W4

Week 4: Written Feedback from Committee Due Along with Selection of the Final Design Concept

Once the art consultant or art project manager has the committee's feedback, they will need to collate it and confirm which is the approved design concept. It is possible that the committee may request some amendments to the final design concept at this stage, so an outline will need to be made of these for the artist, including any comments on colours, size, materials and conceptual direction. There must also be a record of why these comments have been made. This outline will be the feedback the art consultant or art project manager will provide to the selected artist.

Week 4: Feedback Call to Art Consultant

If the project is being run by an art project manager and an art consultant, then this is the time for the consultant to be briefed on the committee's feedback. They will then contact the artist that has been chosen for the project and let them know of the committee's decision and pass on the feedback. (If the project is run by an art project manager only, then they will need to call the artist to do this.)

Week 4: Feedback Call to the Selected Artist

At this point, the art project manager or art consultant will need to contact the artist that has been chosen for the project. This should be done by phone and then followed up with a confirmation email. Feedback and any suggested revisions or amendments should also be detailed at this time, both by phone and in writing. The artist should be allowed at least one week (and up to ten days) to make revisions.

It is also important to establish here that the artist is still available and on board for the project, and nothing has changed with their circumstances. I have seen some artists take on too much and then decide they no longer want to do the project. Also, it is best to confirm your selected artist's commitment to the project before rejecting the other artists. That way if your first choice is no longer on board, you have other options to select from.

Week 4: Feedback Call to the Artists Not Selected

Once the selected artist has been confirmed, the unsuccessful applicants will need to be informed by phone. Here is when the committee's feedback should be communicated to each artist and delivered in a constructive and positive way. These conversations will need to be followed up with an email so that each artist has the feedback in writing.

NOTE: At Art Pharmacy, we believe it is best practice to pay for the design concept work done by the artists not selected. The amount paid for this work could be anything from $300 to $5000 depending on the project and the level of the concepts. We ask the artists to invoice us and we pay them quickly, usually within two weeks. This shows that we support their practice and that we appreciate them even though they weren't taken on for the project. We recommend that this best-practice approach be taken on by all who run an art project.

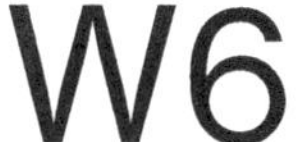

Week 6: Selected Artist's Amended Concepts Due

The selected artist resubmits their revised design concept for review so that the art consultant or art project manager can check if the committee's suggested amendments have been taken into consideration.

Week 6: Committee Meeting 2
– Review of Amended Design Concept (Round 2)

The art consultant or art project manager meet with the art committee to review the amended design concept. If possible, the committee will sign off on the final concept at this point.

NOTE: If the committee needs even more time or has more feedback here, notes should be taken and the feedback provided to the artist so they can make further amendments. A due date for these amendments must also be given to the artist – preferably within two weeks – and a new committee meeting date set for a Round 3 review of the design concept.

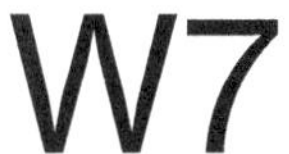

Week 7: Confirm the Concept with
the Artist and Issue the Contract

Once the design concept has been approved, the contract for the artist should be issued and the artist provided with an opportunity to review it before signing. As a general guide, the contract should be issued to the artist around one or two weeks after the approval of the concept, and the artist be allowed one to two weeks to review it. (Note that the timing of the issue and signing of the contract will vary from project to project, and will depend on when the concept is approved.) Once the artist has signed the contract, it is good practice to provide them with an indication of when you'll need their invoices (their fee will be paid in instalments) and to let them know when they can expect to be paid.

NOTE: Until the artist brief is incorporated into the contract, it remains open to changes and review, so it needs to be kept up to date. The contract itself, however, should be prepared in advance so that it can be issued to the artist when the design concept has been approved.

W8 Week 8: Artist to Submit Signed Contract and Commence Work

When the artist has signed the contract and all the paperwork has been done, the artist can get to work. The time they will have to create the artwork will depend on the project. This is often between four and eight weeks but can be longer for larger or complex artworks.

Weeks 8 to 12: Other Work for the Art Project to Commence

During this time, the art consultant or art project manager will commence work on other details of the project that need to be organised, such as looking into artwork framing if required, writing content for and organising the artwork plaque, booking a photographer and videographer to document the artwork (and sometimes the process, if the artist is comfortable with this), sending the artist WHS documents to fill out, etc. Now is also a good time to start organising and refining installation day.

NOTE: If you intend to use a photographer or videographer to document anything to do with the artwork for marketing or publicity purposes – for example, the artist's progress or the installation – the artist must be informed very clearly that this will happen. It is best to include information about this in the brief and in the artist's contract.

W12 Week 12: Completion of the Artwork

The artist will be expected to have the artwork finished on the agreed due date, which should be well before installation day. The artwork will need to be viewed by the art consultant or art project manager to ensure that the artwork delivers on expectations. Depending on where the artist (or the fabricator of the artwork) is located, a site visit is advisable, otherwise the artist will need to submit high-quality photographs of the artwork for final approval. Verbal approval will need to be followed up by an email to make sure all involved are happy with the outcome. The artwork can then be signed off by the art project manager and/or the art consultant.

NOTE: While I have this at Week 12 here, which provides four weeks for the artist in this example to create the artwork, the artist may need up to 12 weeks to complete the artwork, depending on its complexity and the project.

W13 Week 13: Second Site Visit with the Artist

Once the artwork is completed and approved, it is useful to schedule another site visit by the artist and the art consultant or art project manager to resolve any issues regarding the artwork or installation. This is also a great opportunity to talk in greater detail with the artist to see how they went with the work, and to reflect on any last changes to the schedule that may be needed.

NOTE: Here is when the art consultant or art project manager should start collating WHS certificates, insurance for the site and a running sheet for installation day. It is important to gather this information early on so the consultant or project manager is prepared for the artwork's installation and is able to communicate information around this to others involved in the project when needed. It is vital to keep everyone who is directly contributing to the art project in the loop regarding the artwork's installation.

W14 Weeks 14 to 16: Work to Commence on the Art Project's Internal Processes

Here is when the art consultant or art project manager will need to start work on the production schedule, ensure all required paperwork has been collated (such as WHS documents, insurance information, etc.), all contracts related to delivery and installation have been signed, and that the artist (and art consultant, if one is used on the job) has been paid for invoices submitted to date.

Weeks 14 to 16: Weekly Check-in with all Parties Involved in the Installation

The art consultant or art manager will need to continually check that all paperwork is up to date and accurately reflects the project, and that things are on track for installation. This will involve confirming all necessary site passes, checking and rechecking the production schedule, contacting security to ensure there is clearance and support on installation day, and checking the weather forecast. Yes, this is important! If there is wet weather predicted, then additional materials or procedures may need to be organised for the installation.

W16 Week 16: Installation Day

It is always advisable to start early on installation day. The art consultant or art project manager will need to ensure that all traffic management is taken care of and underway, and the production team and installers are ready to go, especially if the work is being installed in the public realm. The photographer and/or videographer (organised around Week 8) should be onsite to capture the moment of installation.

The client (the commissioning body), and the art project manager or art consultant will need to be onsite a few days prior, on the day of installation and visit a few days after to manage any problems and queries.

Week 16: Inspecting the Installed Artwork

It is paramount that the artwork be inspected within 24 hours of installation. At the end of the installation stage, the artwork should be ready for inspection for final approval by the client, the art project manager and/or art consultant and the art committee. If everyone is happy, the work can be signed off.

NOTE: Once the project is signed off, the artist should issue their final invoice for the remainder of their fee. If the artwork will be publicised, the marketing and PR teams should start work on this now.

While this sample timeline of a four-month project might seem detailed, it is more of a rough draft of what to expect. You may encounter delays around feedback, contracts or meetings. If the site is not ready, you may have to delay the installation date. However, if you have a clear timeline set in advance (and included in the project's brief) that all parties are aware of, you will be more likely to keep things on track.

Installation

Your artist brief should include details for installation of the artwork, such as site access and services available. For example, if the artwork is to go into the lobby of the building, the artist will not only need to ensure it will fit into the space, but also determine if the artwork can be taken into the space as one large work or if it will need be delivered in pieces that are then assembled onsite. Or if the artwork requires electricity (in the case of a digital artwork), they'll need to determine if there is a suitable power outlet at the site or whether they'll need to request for one to be installed in advance.

Similarly, include a point here for the artist to consider the lighting for the artwork in the space. This is something that is often forgotten or left to the last minute.

Additional information around any mandatory paperwork required to work on the site should also be part of the artist brief. This includes:

- WHS guidelines
- expected level of insurance
- an outline of any necessary equipment for visiting the site, such as a hard hat or appropriate footwear
- an indication of whether the site will be complete at time of installation or still under construction
- an outline of the expected condition of the site after the artist has completed installation of the artwork.

While you and your team may be used to dealing with this sort of paperwork, the artist may not be. It is important to allow the artist adequate time to work through what may be unfamiliar documents to ensure they are prepared for installation.

Covering these installation details in the early stages can prevent delays and extra expenses down the track.

Budget

Giving the artist a budget to work towards and making their fees clear is another very important part of the brief.

Once you have included all the information we've looked at in this chapter in your artist brief and it has been signed off by the art committee, you are ready to engage the right artist or artists for your project. With a detailed and clear brief, you will be able to give the artist everything they will need to know about what you want for your art project. They'll be able to take the brief and use it to create a selection of design concepts to present to you and your art committee for review, selection and approval.

GOLDEN POINTS

01 The artist brief is created before engaging an artist. All key information the artist will need, including the art narrative, must be incorporated into the brief. Be clear and concise, and include only relevant information.

02 Remember to include full site details, a site visit for the artist, a clear design concept direction, a timeline, information regarding installation and the budget.

DESIGN CONCEPTS AND CONCEPT DIRECTION
This is a really important chapter! Having the artist/s create design
concepts inspired by the brief is the most important step you can take in
getting the right artwork on your site. This process is a way of testing the
waters with your artist before fully engaging them on the project. If you
are yet to select an artist, then you may also carry out this test with a few
different artists from your shortlist before deciding on who you will employ.
In this scenario, this process is known as a 'design competition'. If you
intend to work this way at your concept development stage, it is best
to make the artists aware of the competitive nature of the process.

It takes time for an artist to come up with a series of design concepts.
Always ensure you pay them for their work, even if you don't choose any
of their options. Do not expect them to do this work for free. If you engage
more than one artist to submit concepts, make sure that all artists are paid
for this preliminary work, preferably on delivery of the design concepts.

Keep in mind that it is best practice for this design concept fee to be
agreed upon before the artists delivers the options – this will help you
maintain good relationships with the artists you interact with. In your fee
agreement, outline what it will include – for example, if the artists are
required to revise or amend their design concept or concepts, or if the
brief changes for some reason, specify how this is taken into account
in the design concept fee and outline what additional renumeration they
can expect for any extra work they may be required to do.

What is a Design Concept?
Essentially, a design concept is a drawing, diagram or sketch of the
artwork the artist proposes for your project. This proposal should
also include an artist bio; a concept statement (more on this shortly);
information on the materials, colours and size of the artwork,
including measurements; and project delivery dates.

The artist's design concepts should
clearly illustrate their idea and be
something that you can show anyone
in your organisation and have them
understand what the artist intends
to create, regardless of that person's
level of art knowledge.

I can't stress how important this design concept stage is to your art project. The initial design concepts are what go to the art committee for review and approval. If the art committee is happy and approve a concept at this stage, then the project can go ahead from this point. Once the committee signs off on a design concept, the artist's contract can be drawn up and the artist can begin work.

However, if you or your art committee are not quite happy with the proposed artwork at this early concept stage, we recommend you **suggest amendments, or review the art narrative and rework the brief to make it clearer for the artist.** In many cases, if the artist's design concepts aren't right it means the art narrative wasn't nailed in the first place. Reviewing the narrative and brief gives the artist an opportunity to do a second round of design concepts that could better reflect what you want to see.

For projects with many stakeholders involved, such as council or government, I recommend choosing at least two or three artists and requesting they provide at least two concepts each. This means that when you present the design concepts to the art committee, you can offer them a larger range of choices. This also gives you a backup if something prevents the artist you've chosen from completing the job – you'll have another concept and artist ready to go so you and your team won't have to start the selection process all over again.

When the design concept has been approved, ensure that it is incorporated into the artist's contract, along with other essentials such as the brief, timeline and budget outline.

Design Concept Direction

As part of the artist brief, you will need to include design concept direction. While the art narrative will form part of this, as well as the information on the project's site, intended location of the work and any physical parameters around size, it is useful for the artist to know what else they'll need to address and how many concepts they'll need to provide. As suggested before, they should provide at least two but preferably three options. This will give the art committee choices, and if they can't settle on one concept, they could then compare the various options and perhaps ask the artist to combine elements of each. Having a variety of design concepts can be a great way to help a committee decide on the strongest art outcome.

Design concept direction also involves you asking the artist to provide the following information about the proposed artwork:

- a clear indication of the materials they intend to use; for example, wood, metal, paint, spray paints (if the work is a mural), etc.
- details of the size of the work. This will depend on the site and location of the artwork. Having the artist provide the size of the artwork will allow you to check they have taken the location of the project into consideration
- an outline of the colours they intend to use. Ask them to be specific about their colour choices and how they intend to use them in the artwork. In some cases, such as a mural, you could request them to provide you with a colour chart
- a breakdown of the costs and how these adhere to the budget you have set for the project.

Once the artist has the brief, which includes the design concept direction, I suggest you allow up to three weeks for them to come up with some design concepts, depending on how complex the expected artwork will be. If you are working on a masterplan development with a council, you might be able to allow them more time here – perhaps four to six weeks – but generally, two to three weeks is enough. It is preferable to get the design concepts to your art committee early on in the project so that the artist who is selected will have time to make amendments if necessary. Getting resolved concepts approved and signed off as soon as possible is the goal – this way, your project timeline should run smoothly and the project will be easier to keep on track.

It will help the artist if you provide an outline of what you expect around delivery of their design concepts. Following is an example of how you could word this:

Your design concepts are due at 9 am on (insert date). Please email them to me at (insert email address). Please submit the following:

- two design concepts saved as jpeg files with a minimum resolution of 300 dpi. This can be a digitally rendered image or a scan of a hand-drawn sketch; each concept must clearly show the colour, materials and composition of your proposed artwork
- a concept statement of 300 to 500 words explaining the concept behind your artwork, including how it relates to the art narrative and other relevant information provided to you in the brief
- a mock-up of your artwork as you see it in the site. Please show this on the site render file provided to you so that we can see it in context. This file will need to be emailed as a jpeg with a minimum resolution of 300 dpi

– your preliminary technical notes. Include any notes on lighting, either for installation or for the artwork itself, and whether you require power or water at the site for installation.

Note that on some projects, the artist's design concepts will be included in the development application. If this is the case, the project may experience a delay, so it is best to factor this into the project timeline and communicate this to all involved, including the artist.

Design Concepts vs Concept Statements

Part of what the artist will be expected to deliver for each design concept is a concept statement. The concept statement differs from the design concept – the design concept illustrates the physical aspect of the artwork, usually through a sketch, drawing or digitally rendered image, but **the concept statement is the idea or theme behind the artwork**. This will relate to the art narrative you provide to the artist in the artist brief. This is another reason why it is so important to have a strong art narrative.

Thinking conceptually about the meaning of a work is a skill that artists excel at – it is what drives their artwork forward. The artist/s you work with will take your art narrative into account and use it to build a concept statement for each design concept they create for you. Alternatively, you may ask the artist to create one concept statement they can use to inspire two or three design concepts. The first option offers a bit more variety and the second generally produces designs that are more focused. Think about what your project needs and let the artist know what you prefer.

Other Considerations

Lighting

At Art Pharmacy, we often work with a lighting designer to help highlight artworks, especially on larger developments. Lighting an artwork properly will make it come alive and draw the viewer to it. This really is a very important factor for the success of your art project – a poorly lit artwork can undermine the success of the outcome. I encourage you to consider using a lighting consultant to help you do this.

If you do, then once the concept has been approved, it is beneficial for the artist and lighting designer to meet and discuss the work. This will help you with planning the installation of both the artwork and the lighting. Even if you don't hire a consultant, I strongly recommend you and your team consider how best to light the artwork, and to do this early on in the timeline so this important aspect of the project is not left to the last minute.

Practical Considerations

Once the artist has delivered the design concepts to you, it is useful to think about the practical considerations of how the proposed artwork will work in the site. For example:

- What are the sightlines to the artwork? Can you see it when you walk in the front door or entrance? If not, where can you see it from?
- How will people move around the artwork? Does it have space around it to allow viewing from multiple angles?
- If the artwork is located on a wall, will it protrude from the surface? If so, how much? Could this be a concern? If so, what can be done to remedy this?
- What other artworks or important features are near the proposed location of the artwork? Will they compete with or complement the artwork?

Artist Engagement

Once the design concept has been approved and signed off by you and your art committee, you are ready to formally engage the artist. It's at this point that the contract will need to be finalised and signed by all parties. Remember to include the art narrative, the brief and the approved design concept in the contract. Include details of any insurance the artist will need, especially for when they work on the site.

At this time, you should also clearly outline the budget to the artist and the fee they will be paid, as well as a schedule of expected delivery times and payments. The overall fee will be paid in instalments, so ensure that you and the artist are clear on how much each instalment will be and when it will be paid.

If you and/or the art committee have any further feedback following the approval of the final design concept, then this is the time to share that with the artist.

GOLDEN POINTS

01 Give clear design concept direction in the brief – explain to the artist what you expect from the artwork with regard to materials, size and timeline.

02 Ask the artist to provide relevant information for each design concept – a concept statement, an illustration of the artwork, indication of the materials, colours and size, and how it will sit in the space.

03 Remember that creating design concepts takes time so pay the artist for this work. Agree on the fee prior to them commencing the work.

04 Take lighting of the artwork into consideration.

SELECTING THE ARTIST

After you have prepared the artist brief and ironed out the essential details of the project, it is time to select an artist. There are various ways to go about selecting the right artist/s for your project, but in each case, it is useful to start with a longlist of options, whittle it down to a shortlist and then make your final selection.

Putting a longlist together can be done via an open or closed expression of interest (EOI) but I believe the best way to do this is to have an art consultant help you because this is what they do best. Your art consultant will provide you with considered options for your longlist and check the availability of each artist and their interest in the project. Once you and your team have settled on a shortlist, you can begin to make your selection of artists who will provide you with concepts inspired by the brief.

Regardless of how you go about it, this is an exciting part of your art project journey as you will be sharing each stage of the selection process with your art project manager, your art committee (if you have one) and possibly other interested stakeholders. Here is often the first reveal of art content you will be reviewing together after all the preliminary work has been done (getting the committee together, finalising the art narrative and writing the brief). Selecting the artist is the next important stage in your art project.

I firmly believe that when selecting the artist you will work with, you should pick someone who aligns with your organisation's values and how you envision the art to be in the intended space. Doing this will ensure that you have an artist on board that understands the core goals of your project, and who will come up with concepts that will answer your project's art narrative. Remember the art dating idea I talked about earlier? Here is where you should look for marriage material.

While I will mostly focus here on having an art consultant help you make your artist selection, let's take a brief look at the other options also.

Open Expressions of Interest (EOI)

The EOI process throws the playing field open to the public. By using this method, you are giving details of the project, with certain criteria that need to be met for eligibility to enter, out to the public so that anyone who is interested can apply.

In this process, the project's background and some of the brief's details are made publicly available through various avenues, such as the local council's website, your art consultant's database, posts on local community Facebook pages, art associations, regional art galleries and articles in art news pages. You'll need to provide enough information about the project so that artists can develop a response, and you'll also need to outline what you would like to see in their response. For example, you can request they include a short biography, photographs of past works, an artist statement and the artist's availability. At this stage, the information you provide and receive will be somewhat general in nature – you should not expect the artist to produce researched designs in answer to a brief without a fee.

Whether you choose this method will really depend on the amount of time and resources you have available. A public EOI tends to be fairer but also requires you to give feedback to all applicants. This could be time-consuming if you get hundreds of applications (which is usually the case for us at Art Pharmacy). You'd have to evaluate each application against set criteria. For example, is the artist based locally, nationally or internationally? What is their previous work like? What other clients have they worked with? Have they answered the art narrative effectively? Given this, each application can take half a day or longer to review. And remember, you'll have to meet with your art committee to do these reviews.

On the other hand, if you don't get many responses to your open EOI, you may be left with a small pool of artists to select from.

Closed EOI

While similar to an EOI made open to the public, in a closed EOI, the details about the project are shared only with a select list of artists who are asked to nominate a response, or who opt into being considered by providing their bio, CV and examples of previous works.

Using an Art Consultant to Create a Researched Artist List

A researched artist list is how an art consultant would approach artist selection, and how I typically end up working with clients for many of Art Pharmacy's projects. I strongly believe using an art consultant at this stage is the best way to find the right artist for the job.

I'll use Art Pharmacy as an example consultancy here. Based on the information provided by the commissioning body – that would be you and your organisation – we would research several artists in our network using the extensive database we've built up over the years via our industry knowledge. Then we'll put together a longlist of artists we think would be suitable for your project.

This list would then go to you, your project team and the art committee to review. Once you have selected two or three artists to make a shortlist (maybe more), then these artists will be provided with the brief and asked to respond to it by creating at least two or three concepts for you and your committee to choose from. The final artist selection process will go on from there.

The way I like to approach creating a handpicked and thoughtful artist selection is to look at what your project requires. In some cases, that will be a selection of artists who have ties to your location; in others, it may be a list that includes artists from diverse backgrounds, or with diverse art practices. It may be both. I believe this is what you should be aiming for if you want to have an original and thoughtful artwork made for your project. Your art consultant can avoid selecting artists that are used on lots of projects, meaning your project will stand out from what, in terms of public art, can be a homogenous city. Variety in the selection is key.

I always ask my clients to consider local artists first and foremost. From a practical point of view, supporting local talent is not only a sustainable approach but it will make the process of working with your artist easier. It may also mean that the artist you choose could have a closer connection to your site than an artist who lives across the country or overseas. In addition, you will be supporting a member of the creative community in your city or local government area.

It is true that working with a national or international artist with a high profile provides a platform for promoting creativity in a way that already carries cultural cache. However, for every high-profile artist that is used, I'd like to see an opportunity being created for an emerging artist. This is not only a responsible approach to take but also a way for you to give back to your community. And remember, supporting local talent can become a great PR story for your project.

The Artist Longlist

I recommend having a longlist of at least four to 12 artists, depending on the requirements of your site, how many art opportunities you can provide and how many art placements you may need. If you are using an art consultant, they can help you decide this and will then develop a list of artists that can cater to your requirements.

I encourage the inclusion of local and diverse artists on corporate and development art projects. My preferred method for putting a varied artist list together is to include artists from culturally and linguistically diverse (CALD) backgrounds, First Nations artists, LGBTIQ+ artists, artists with or examining disability, and artists who use diverse methods in their works. This may include artists who work with a variety of mediums and styles producing artworks such as paintings, sculptures, furniture, digital art and more.

It is best to provide your art consultant with as much specific information about the art project as you can, particularly the art narrative and the brief. This will be very helpful to them in making a targeted list. It will also put you in a strong place; a list that focuses on your narrative will give you and your art committee lots of suitable choices, and will get you thinking of the possible concepts each artist could offer.

When I make a list, I include each artist's name, a short biography and their headshot, as well as a wide selection of their previous work to provide the client with a good idea of the artist's range. I find that in the research phase of the longlist, it is important to ask each artist what styles they are currently working in, or if there are directions they are keen to explore further. What I don't want to do is present my client with examples of the artist's work in a style the artist has moved on from long ago. A great artist is always evolving and growing their practice – like many of us, they change their style over time. Think of your 1990s haircut!

These changes in an artist's work can be obvious and dramatic, or gradual and subtle, so it's always important for an art consultant to speak to their artists before including them and their work on a longlist.

If your art project manager is well versed in art and the local art scene and you don't have an art consultant on board, they should be able to create a longlist for you. And on a related note, if someone within your organisation has suggested an artist to include on the longlist, talk with your art consultant and/or your art project manager and try to include that suggestion if the artist is available. This is only fair, and it promotes equal opportunity and will encourage your team to think about art. Remember: it's important to support people in your organisation who are interested in art – they could be a budding creative pioneer!

Always have Choices

While I am no expert in the field of comparative decision-making, I do know that there are a lot of different processes going on in a person's mind when they are making a decision – mathematical, subjective, neurobiological, evolutionary and cultural. It is important that whatever method of artist selection you use for your project, you have adequate and appropriate choices to select from.

You and your art committee will need to take the time to review each option on your artist longlist, be patient when making your shortlist and carefully consider the frontrunners when making your final selection. There is no need to hire a random artist without first carefully examining all the options.

I use what I call 'the chair analogy' to explain the importance of this to clients. Imagine you are given a chair and are asked, 'Is this a good chair?' You'd be hard pressed to give much feedback. You might say 'Well, it seems like a perfectly good chair … seems to do the trick, I guess.'

Now imagine you are given two very different chairs and asked which chair you prefer. In this new situation you might say, 'I prefer this chair because it's more comfortable than the other one.' Or perhaps you'd say, 'I prefer this one because it is adjustable,' or 'I like this one because of the colour and the fabric', etc. If I observe you doing this, suddenly I have a lot more information on how you make decisions, what's important to you and what your preferences are in relation to aesthetics, design and comfort. With choices, you can learn more about what people like. So … always have choices! They are important to the selection process.

A comparative decision-making model is equally valuable in art. Choice and options are incredibly important in art projects because you are often working with different levels of art fluency, interest, engagement and taste. The selection of an artist, and later a design concept, often comes down to taste. However, it should not only be about that, so ensure you and your team take the time to think through all the options on your artist list before selecting who to go with for design concepts.

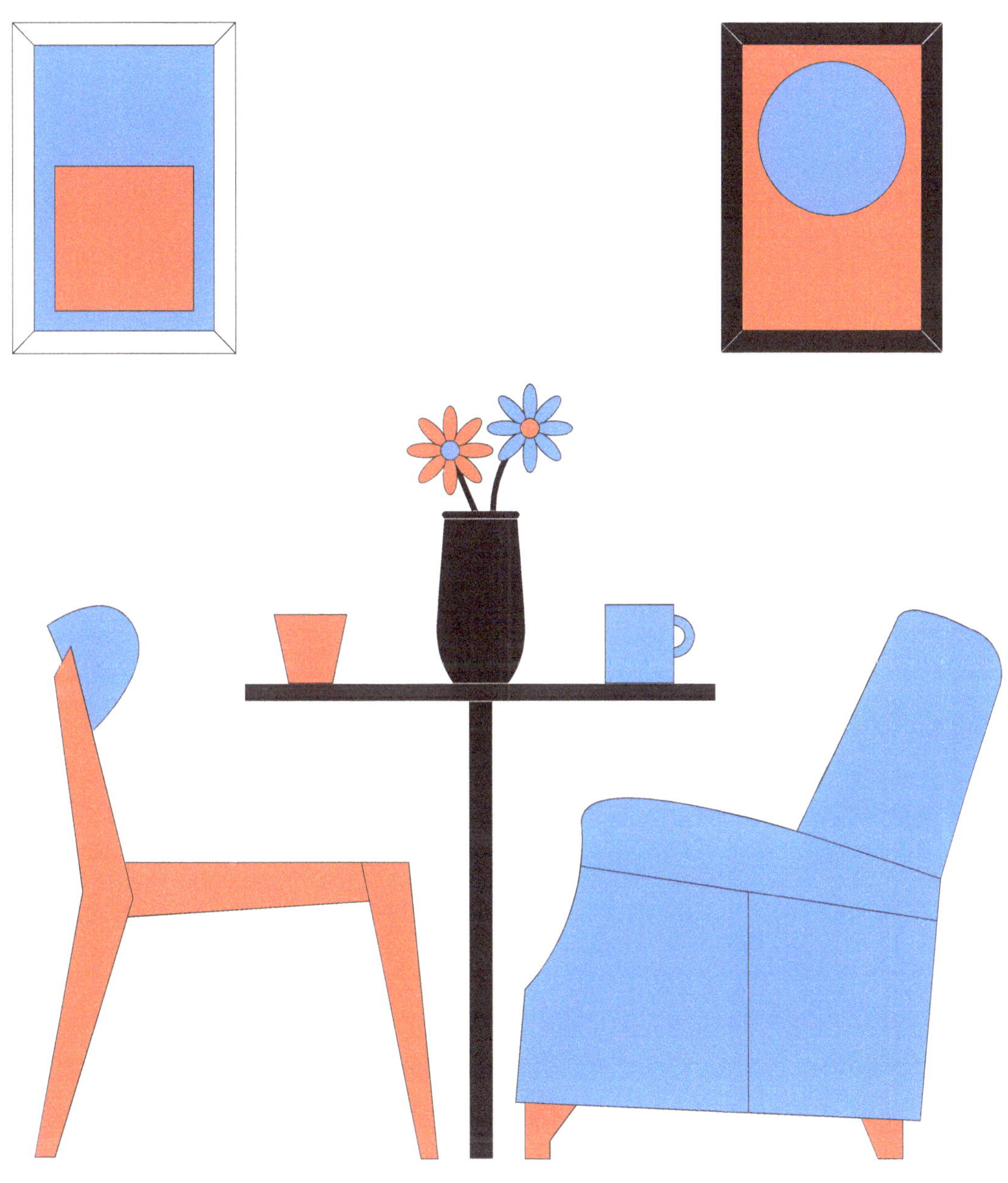

Selecting the Final Design Concept

Being able to compare options is also vital when selecting the design concept that will become the final artwork – always ask your chosen artists to provide at least two design concepts each. Having options here will mean you and your art committee will have a greater likelihood of finding the right artwork for your project, and will be able to provide constructive feedback to the artist to make this happen. For example, your feedback may look a little more like 'I prefer that design to this one because …' rather than a flat 'I don't like it.'

This selection process offers a great opportunity to harvest valuable feedback for the artist. If you are using an art consultant, having them present at your concept selection meeting will help you keep things on track. They'll then be able to communicate your feedback clearly to the artist. If you aren't using a consultant, then you or your art project manager should do this.

Some questions useful to ask during the design concept selection process include:
  - What did you like about the concept?
  - How well did the artist respond to the art narrative?
  - Is the artwork's appearance and theme appropriate
    for the location and the space?
  - Does the size of the artwork suit the space?
    If not, should it be bigger or smaller?
  - Do you like the material?
  - Do the colours work?

Remember to gather feedback on every element of the work, not just bits here and there. This information will help the artist to know what to do if amendments are requested. Give the information to the artist but always keep a copy of it on file so that you can refer back to it later if necessary.

I also recommend that you, your art project manager and your committee provide detailed feedback on all the concepts from all the artists who put forward proposals, not just on the ones you like. This will help you shape any amendments to the artist brief that might be needed.

Artists Attending Committee Meetings

Once you have selected your artist/s, given them the art narrative and brief, and asked them to produce design concepts, the selection process becomes more focused. Generally, you, your art project manager and/or your art consultant will be the ones to pitch the design concepts to your art committee. Recently, though, I have seen a growing trend for clients to request that their selected artist pitch their concepts directly to the art committee. There are pros and cons to this approach.

Pros

In my experience, providing the commissioning body (you) with an opportunity to talk to the artist allows them to get a strong understanding of the concepts the artist puts forward. This can sometimes be more beneficial than leaving it up to your art project manager or art consultant to interpret the artist's concepts for you and your art committee.

Cons

Sometimes artists can be shy, or not very confident when speaking to a group of corporate people. This can detract from the intent of their work and how they present it. Also, if you are inexperienced at dealing with artists, it may be tricky for you and your committee to manage the artists' reactions if the artwork concepts are not warmly received, or require amendments. This can be a downside of having the artist present when their design concepts are being reviewed.

However, if you would like to include the artist in the initial selection meeting (which the artist should be paid to attend), you'll discover that your art consultant is worth their weight in gold as they can plan and action this meeting for you, and help you manage the artist.

After that first meeting, I recommend that any further necessary interaction with the artist be carried out by the art consultant, as this provides one voice and one direct line for both you and the artist to deal with. This is especially useful if you are employing more than one artist on the project.

Synergy

Something else to consider in your choice of artist is how you and your art manager or art consultant interact with them. You will be working closely with the artist during your art project, sometimes communicating with them on a daily or weekly basis, so, it is important to be able to work with them in a collaborative way. You need to see eye to eye with them. If you find that at the beginning of the concept stage things aren't working well, or you are having issues with the artist, then it might be best to choose a different artist. The total timeframe of an art project can be anything from four weeks up to a year in some cases, so you must build a good relationship with the artist early on and develop a synergy with them. Yes, we are back to the handy idea of art dating!

Follow your gut on this – if you have concerns in the early stages before the contract has been signed, either resolve any issues as quickly as possible or consider choosing a different artist. If you are having issues later in the project, always return to the brief and the approved design concepts that were agreed upon and included in the contract. This can be a great help for getting things back on track. And remember: if things aren't quite working in the early stages, you can always review the art narrative – as I've said before, if the design concepts aren't right, then maybe the narrative isn't right. If this is the case, talk to your artist when reviewing this – they are experts at defining and refining art narratives.

If things are really not working after you have engaged the artist and the contract has been signed, you may have to come to an agreement with the artist to part ways. Your art consultant can assist you in handling this delicate situation. For example, if I was to do this, I would set up a meeting with you and the artist where we could outline what your expectations were for the project, what isn't working for you and why. Being open and honest here is key as the artist will want to understand the reasoning behind your decision and be given an opportunity to respond.

If it is only the artist you are having trouble with but still love their artwork concept, then, depending on the project and the contract's terms, you may be able to have a fabricator work with your art consultant to finish the job. The artist will still own the copyright (unless they have sold it to you) and be credited for the work, but the artwork will belong to you. In this scenario, you will need to ensure the artist is paid for the work they have carried out prior to you letting them go.

I have seen many artworks delivered in this way, especially those created by fine artists (traditional painters or artists working on paper) who go on to work in the public art realm. They conceive the artwork but it will go on to be made in steel or bronze by their preferred fabricators (more on these specialists shortly). If you work with an artist who does this, I suggest having them return to the project at the very end to confirm they are happy with the final artwork, prior to the installation phase. This provides a good synergy between the artist, you and the art project team, and ensures everyone is satisfied.

Lastly, if you are having problems with your art consultant rather than the artist, you can also part ways with them if need be. It is good practice here to pay them for the work they have completed to date so that you part amicably. At Art Pharmacy, we have picked up several art consulting jobs where the client was unhappy with their previous consultant, experienced a communication breakdown with them, or where there were no clearly defined processes put in place from the beginning. That's partly why I am writing this book! If you follow the guidelines in this book for your art project, you will minimise the chance of things going pear-shaped.

How to Choose a Fabricator

For some projects, you, your art consultant and the artist may choose to collaborate with a fabricator, particularly if the artwork is a large piece that involves specialist materials or requires complex engineering to put together. Some artists do all their own work, but some leave part or all of their artwork's construction to a fabricator who can help them to realise their design concept.

Fabricators are skilled artists in their own right and can bring diverse expertise to your project. Their skills can inspire you and the artist to expand the ideas for your art project into new mediums. You don't have to spend the next decade learning how to blow glass, weld metal or build holograms – the right fabricator can create work using these techniques for you. Fabricators are adept at realising concepts; they are builders at heart.

There are many fabricators that specialise in different areas and different materials. At Art Pharmacy, we often outsource the construction of a commissioned artwork (in collaboration with the artist) as we know our fabricators can tailor-make the work to the artist's specifications. A good fabricator will understand the aesthetic, philosophical and material issues that drive the artist's concept – this is often a complex and quite profound interaction, both for the artist who works with the fabricator and the art consultant who commissions them.

Choosing a fabricator is similar to how you select your artist – you'll need your art consultant to put forward suggestions, then you'll need to think carefully before making your choice. Always ensure you have the right person with the right skills for the job, and work to develop the right synergy with them. A good relationship with your selected fabricator will give you the best chance of getting a good outcome for the artwork.

GOLDEN POINTS

01 When choosing your artist, always start with a longlist. An art consultant can provide you with a researched artist longlist for you to select from.

02 Consider local artists where possible and look at a diverse range of artists.

03 Ensure the shortlisted artists offer you at least two design concept choices each so you can compare before selecting the final concept.

04 Always give the artist constructive feedback, both positive and negative so they can iron out any issues and learn from the experience.

05 I'll say it again: always have choices!

CONTRACTS

No two public spaces are the same and no two public art commissions will be the same. Therefore, a fit-for-purpose or tailor-made contract between you and each of your suppliers, including the artist, is mandatory. Your contracts also need to be appropriate for the art project in question. Unfortunately, some artist's contracts I've seen have consisted of parts of other contracts cut and pasted together. This is not good practice.

Modifying a contract that's been written for an engineer or a scaffolding supplier to make a contract for your artist isn't going to be right for the project and will likely cause you problems. In the early days of Art Pharmacy, I was once given a 120-page contract for a project where all we were doing was managing a single mural. The contract did not cater to the project at all. You can't put an engineer and an artist in the same category.

If you want to work with an art consultant and artists, then you and your legal team will need to be prepared to work together to form agreements that are fair, reasonable and appropriate. There are many great lawyers working with the arts community who specialise in this. They can help you write a contract that will suit your needs. A great place where you can find further information on this is the Arts Law website.[18]

Generally, I have found that the legal teams of some organisations can take a fair bit of time to write and review contracts, so I suggest you start the process as early as possible. Your project can be easily derailed if the artist is ready to begin work but their contract is still being worked on.

Also, remember to give the artist time to review the contract. Many artists are unfamiliar with this sort of legal documentation. Better yet, have a face-to-face meeting with either the art consultant or artist (preferably both) and walk them through the contract so the artist will understand what they are signing and get a grasp of what your expectations are. Some art consultants or artists will want their own legal representation to check through the contract, so allow time for that as well.

Always ensure that the contract covers everything the artists needs to know about the project and is written in an easily digestible way. The contract should also cover any insurance the artist is required to have. I have professional indemnity insurance and public liability insurance set at $20 million. It is standard for clients to request this from Art Pharmacy, even if it is simply to hang a curated art collection in an office. However, this level of insurance might be too costly for an artist who works on their own. Consider whether a lower level of insurance could be acceptable to reduce this high cost for the artist.

---

18   Arts Law, www.artslaw.com.au

Following are some elements your contract should include:
- the artist's brief, including the art narrative and the project timeline
- information about any planned publicity of the work and expectations around promotion. For example, is the artist allowed to promote their work during the process of making the artwork via social media or other avenues? Is the artist required to be onsite during the installation of the work? Will they be expected to attend events that celebrate the artwork? What other marketing are you expecting the artist to be involved in?

  Note: Events created to publicise the artwork can be a good thing but remember that you will need to pay the artist for their time to attend these. If they live interstate or overseas, then you will need to pay for their travel costs if you want them to attend. This should be outlined in the contract.
- terms around confidentiality, if any are required
- confirmation of who owns the copyright. If the artist is to retain the copyright, make this clear; if you wish to purchase the copyright, make this clear; if you wish to licence the work and intend to pay the artist royalties in addition to their fee, make this clear. These issues are all to do with intellectual property and must be clarified for the artist (and you) in the contract
- the artist's warranty, if you require it. In an artist's warranty, they 'warrant that their work [does] not infringe [on] anyone's rights and … indemnify the commissioner against any claims arising out of their work'.[19] You may not require this, but if you do, put it in the contract
- details of any insurance the artist will need to have that will enable them to work on the site. Be clear about what you expect here, and be fair and reasonable
- details on WHS for the site
- an outline of the fee, payment terms and dates, and the dollar values of the milestone progress payments, including a clear indication of each payment's GST component
- information on the reimbursement of any other expenses that may be incurred and other variables
- information on what you expect around the delivery and installation of the artwork

---

19   Arts Law, Caveat: Visual Artists and Warranties and Indemnities, www.artslaw.com.au/article/caveat-visual-artists-and-warranties-and-indemnities/

- a clause that covers what will happen if the greater project
  is delayed. For example, you may include an offer to provide
  the artist with a retainer until the project is ready to continue
- a clause around terminating the contract if you decide that
  the artist isn't right for the project, including terms of payment
  for work completed
- a clause regarding what happens if the artist moves overseas
  or interstate
- a clause regarding what happens if you and/or the artist decide
  to part ways
- information on how you will relocate or remove the artwork from
  the site should that be required in the future. To avoid infringing
  on the artist's moral rights, the artist would need to agree to allow
  the artwork to be relocated or possibly destroyed (although this
  is unlikely) if it no longer fits its purpose.

The Artist's Fee and Payments

In the early stages of engaging an artist, it is best to clearly outline the
details of how you intend to pay them for the initial concept development.
Send this to the artist in an email so they have it in writing. If you are
asking more than one artist to create concepts, include how they will
be recompensed if their designs are not chosen; let each of them know
these terms. At this stage, your email could also outline the overall payment
schedule so each artist has an idea of what they might expect if they
are chosen for the project.

For example, your email may state that you will pay the artist an initial
fee for concept development. If they are selected to work on the project,
and once one of their design concepts has been approved and finalised,
you may then offer to pay 50% of the artist's total fee up front to cover the
materials they will need and their time. (This is considered best practice.)
Your second progress payment may then consist of a further 25% midway
through the project. The final 25% could then be slated for payment 30 days
after the artwork has been delivered and installed and everyone has agreed
that they are happy with it.

It is also useful to include a little scope within the artist's fee for
any artwork amendments that may be required during the production
of the artwork.

Later, when you have selected the artist and have signed off on the final
concept, the fee and milestone progress payments should be discussed
in greater detail and agreed upon by all parties before being included the
final payment plan in the contract. I strongly recommend including the
payment terms, dates and values of proposed progress payments in the

artist's contract and stipulating them early on. Artists will have ongoing expenses to cover during the timeframe of the project, so they'll need to know how much money is coming in and when. The contract should also cover how the artist will be compensated if there is any change of project direction or timeline.

Larger organisations tend to offer a 60 day turnaround for payment, but for small businesses or freelancers – such as your artist – 30 days is preferable. In recent years, the Business Council of Australia has developed the Australian supplier payment code.[20] Partaking in the code is voluntary, but I encourage you to do this as it ensures small business suppliers are paid promptly. This goes a long way to easing financial stress and supporting good cash flow.

Always explain to the artist how your organisation's payment system works, and how and when you expect the artist to invoice you for the project. Put them in touch with your accounts department at the beginning of the project so they know who to contact and how to prepare their invoices.

---

20   Business Council of Australia,
www.bca.com.au/supplier_payment_code

          THE PROJECT STEPS

GOLDEN POINTS

01 Employ a specialist arts lawyer to write the artist's contract. Don't try to retrofit a contract that is suited to other suppliers. It needs to be fit for purpose.

02 Start the development of the contract with your legal team early in the piece.

03 Discuss payment terms and milestone payment timings up front and be clear who the artist should send their invoices to.

INSTALLATION DAY AND POST-INSTALLATION DEBRIEF

Once the project has been completed, carrying out a debrief about the successes and failures of the project with the project team will offer you a lot of insight into the process and provide you with information on what you can do better next time.

Art projects consist of a practical series of tasks that need to be undertaken but they are also an expression of the art narrative you want to communicate to your audience or community. A debrief should cover both areas and allow you and your team to reflect on how the project was carried out.

This debrief meeting doesn't have to be long – one hour should be enough. Make sure all the people who were involved in the project are free to attend as you should have everyone onboard for this. Some of the questions you might discuss include:

- Was the project a challenge to undertake?
  If so, what were the specific challenges?
- What was easy? Why was it easy?
- Was the project delivered on time?
- Was the budget sufficient?
- What feedback has the project received, formal or otherwise?
- What media or social media coverage did the project receive?
  What are people saying?
- Were the expected outcomes met by the project?
  If not, in what way did the project fail to deliver?
  What can be done to improve on this next time?
- Are we all proud of this? Why or why not?
- What can be done better next time?

If you have established that metrics or measurable outcomes are important to your decision-makers, then review these during the debrief as well.

Learning to work with creatives is a skill to master and takes time. The information you glean from the debrief process will be invaluable reference for your next art project. However, so often the golden crumbs of experience that get shaken out of this reflection process are lost or not made available to the rest of the organisation. Always document what you learn in the debrief process. Measuring and recording both the successes and issues of your art project will help you and your colleagues when undertaking future art projects. You may wish to create a manual using the questions above to outline the learnings you gained on the project, cover all the procedures you implemented and detail those you would implement if you were to do a similar project in the future.

For every project Art Pharmacy works on, we make a list of issues we encountered and note down the steps that we took to resolve them. Then, if required, we update our processes and policies in order to limit the chance of those issues arising again. This is vital information that we can refer to time and time again. I encourage you to create a similar record of your own art project.

Share your Learnings
Creative projects require specialist knowledge and experience to undertake successfully. It is very useful to share these learnings with your team. You shouldn't overlook the opportunity to develop specialist knowledge within your own organisation.

Even if you choose to engage an external art project manager or consultant, you or your art project manager will be better placed to provide clear guidance with the benefit of what you have learnt on a previous art project, especially in the context of your specific organisation and the unique challenges and opportunities it might face.

So, along with documenting your art project, remember to make that document available and easy to access – you never know who in your organisation might be involved in a future art project.

GOLDEN POINT

01 Always have a debrief after the project with the whole team so you can capture the golden crumbs of knowledge you've learnt. These can be used for next time.

TROUBLESHOOTING

All the creative projects I have been involved in have been very different from each other. In my experience, most projects are likely to have a few hiccups or will need things ironed out, so I tend to expect a few surprises along the way. Different organisations, different teams, unique site challenges and unanticipated issues are a part of what my job entails. My team and I work through these issues together – we are creative problem-solvers working on projects that require skill and patience.

Many problems that can occur at the pointy end of the project are mitigated by doing the groundwork: developing a strong project narrative, a detailed artist brief and a solid contract. Having these in place should prevent many possible issues in advance. Including a little extra in the project's budget for the unforeseeable is also a good idea.

Due to the nature of creative projects, it can be hard to predict what could go wrong, but I have put together the following outline of possible problem areas to give you a guide. I've structured this around some of the challenging lessons I've learnt while running an art consultancy business. I admit I've made a few mistakes in the past, so hopefully this information will help you avoid making the same ones!

I've also included here a few things you can do after the installation phase that will help you review and record your learnings for any future art projects you might undertake.

Issues arising on projects can be categorised into three main areas:
- the groundwork phase
- the design concept phase
- the installation phase.

THE GROUNDWORK PHASE

People   **Issue:** The person managing the project has left and the new person wants to be brought up to date.

Solution: People move on. This is a fact of life. Always consider key person risk when choosing your art project manager. It is important to always have at least two people across the project, whether that be your art project manager and an art consultant, or your art consultant and one of the members of your art committee, or some other combination. The golden rule here is to **always have at least two key people who understand the project in its entirety**. To help these key people, and anyone new who comes onto the project, remember to keep all relevant documents up to date, available and accessible. This includes your art strategy and art narrative, the artist brief, the artist's contract (if you are up to that stage) and the project timeline.

Heritage Sites **Issue:** You're working on a heritage site. It's tricky and the work is taking longer than you expected.

Solution: Working on a heritage site can be difficult because they usually have more constraints than other sites, and many planning laws that need to be adhered to. There are always special considerations to take into account before, during and after the job. Get started early to mitigate any issues. During the groundwork phase, find the right heritage consultants to help you identify any potential issues as soon as possible. Ask in advance where you can place artwork that will be low on impact, or find out if there have been other artworks that have already been used previously and where they were placed. This will reduce the impact your artwork will make by reusing an existing approved location on the site.

When working with government heritage buildings, try to get support from the government's internal team rather than engaging an external consultant. You will get a better understanding of what is possible if you can use a heritage consultant who has experience with the building or has come recommended by the people who know the building.

No Art Narrative **Issue:** You skipped the art narrative stage because you thought it might save time but are now unhappy with the design concepts developed by the artist you've selected.

Solution: Don't skip the art narrative stage! Doing this will never save you time in the long run. It is vital your project has a strong art narrative. This ties your organisation's values and mission together and provides a theme for the artist to use as inspiration. It explains the why of your project, acts as an overarching guide in the selection of the artwork and will inform the outcome of the project.

Always have a preliminary meeting with your art committee to go through the art narrative. This will help you select the right artists and help them provide you with the right design concepts. Without an art narrative, you will get design concepts that you weren't expecting. Developing a strong art narrative is a process that will mitigate you getting an undesirable result. So please don't skip this step – it is essential.

Art Committee is Sending Mixed Messages

Issue: You have two art committees that are providing conflicting information to your art manager or art consultant.

Solution: It is tempting for large organisations or councils who manage multiple stakeholders to overcomplicate things. On a few projects, Art Pharmacy has had to deal with two different art committees. In this sort of situation, when we share a longlist of artists with Committee Number 1 and they make some choices, someone on Committee Number 2 is likely to disagree. This can be time-consuming and counterproductive. The same applies for a committee with a lot of people on it. Decisions are not made efficiently when there are too many people involved.

Avoid having two committees and keep your art committee small – four to six people are plenty. If you must have two committees, let your art project manager or consultant know about this in advance so they can prepare for the challenges this might entail. They will need to keep dates of decisions that are made and a record of who makes them. This is vital to ensure everyone and everything stays on track, including expected deliverables.

Short Timeframe

Issue: You've employed an art consultant halfway through the job and they are now pressed for time to complete the work.

Solution: If you are going to use an art consultant, make sure you give them enough time to work on your art project. Art Pharmacy has often been brought onto projects that have short timeframes – usually jobs that involve curating art for corporate offices or lobby spaces. This has sometimes happened for public art projects as well and we've been left scrambling to get things done.

We can't stress how important it is to engage your art consultant as early as possible so they have enough time to plan and advise. It is best to commission the art consultant at the same time as you commission the architect you'll use on the project as their roles go hand in hand; artwork placemaking can be integrated into your site at the same time as the architect designs it. The architect and art consultant will work collaboratively towards a common goal.

An associated mistake that I see repeatedly is that the selection of art for a site is an afterthought. This then leads to an artist and art consultant being brought into the project at its later stages, resulting in a host of other problems. It is counterintuitive to fit existing artwork into a site rather than giving an artist the opportunity to create something original that will work with the space.

THE DESIGN CONCEPT PHASE

Variation in Concept Delivery

Issue: Your chosen artist is unable to render their design concepts in a way you expect.

Solution: Artists have different ways of delivering their design concepts, ranging from hand-drawn illustrations to digital files. Some artists are great at using digital programs like Adobe Photoshop or Illustrator to mock-up their concepts, but some may not have the skills to render their ideas in a digital format, as usually required in a project. This can lead to a difference in appearance of the final artwork to the original design concept, one that you may not have expected or been prepared for.

Please be open and accepting of the fact that all artists will have a different level of skill for rendering their ideas, especially if you are working with multiple artists on a project. In a larger group, the skill level for this task will vary greatly.

If the artist can't render their final concept in a digital format and you don't feel confident of the outcome with a hand-drawn design, then I suggest you engage a graphic designer to do the render so there is no room for error. Ensure that the artist and designer understand one another, as the designer will be the artist's interpreter in this context – together, they must be able to realise the artist's vision of the design concept.

The Design Concepts are Unsatisfactory

Issue: You are unhappy with the concepts developed by the artist or artists you have selected.

Solution: Go back to the art narrative and rethink the brief. See if you can refine it or add detail and offer feedback to the artist. It is important to give them an opportunity to make amendments. Workshop the narrative if necessary and bring the artist in on this process – they can help you with this.

The Artist's Photographs of the Artwork are Inadequate

Issue: The artist provides you with unclear, damaged, low-resolution or pixelated photographs of the final artwork.

Solution: When requesting photos of the artwork from the artist, always specify what resolution and file format you expect. Tell the artist you need high-resolution images that show the artwork as a whole and from different angles – give them some guidance and they should be able to deliver what you expect.

THE INSTALLATION PHASE

Hanging-System Issues

Issue: Your artwork is a sculpture that needs to hang from the ceiling, but there is no hanging system included in the fit-out plan.

Solution: When fitting out a specific area – for example, a lobby or several locations on a site for a corporate art collection – always consider how the artworks will be presented in the space. You don't want a boom lift coming into your freshly fitted-out lobby to install an engineered hook that should have been installed weeks ago.

There are many hanging systems available on the market so it is best for yours to be included in the plan by the architect or interior designer. However, if you are installing artwork in an existing site, there may be a variety of systems already there – meaning they may not integrate with one another. Examine these early on and update them if need be.

If it is a new site, the hanging system or art rails you use should be researched, chosen and installed well ahead of artwork installation time. Remember to compare options on hanging systems as you will need to find one that will suit your artwork or artworks. Also, once you settle on a system, you will likely work with the company that produces it well into the future – most of these systems do not integrate with one another so it is not easy to change suppliers. It pays to find a good supplier who will understand the site, is professional to deal with and responsive to your needs – especially if you are planning on moving the artworks around on a regular basis, as you might do with a corporate art collection.

Unpredictable Occurrences Onsite

Issue: The area for installation is not as you expect it to be, or your installation team can't access the area. For example:
- an electrical panel was installed in the middle of the wall where a large artwork needs to go
- the lift isn't wide enough for the artwork or they are out of service
- an access ramp that wasn't on the original plans has been installed in front of a wall where a mural was to be painted. You now need a boom lift for the artist, but the artist doesn't have a licence to work one
- the wall where a mural is to go has not been adequately prepared
- not enough site access cards have been provided to you and your team

> — you are told at the last minute that the artist
> is only allowed to work on the site after hours
> — the security team and the project managers
> were not made aware of installation day,
> so the installation team was turned away.

Solution: All of these issues are easily fixed by pre-empting them. Always go through your installation checklist, always makes sure that everyone involved is aware of the installation date and time, check and recheck everything beforehand and, if possible, do a few site visits before installation day so you can see the site. This will reduce the number of surprises you may encounter on installation day.

Inadequate Preparation of Walls for a Mural Application

Issue: The wall for your mural is still in a raw concrete state or there has only been one coat of paint applied.

Solution: Raw concrete is very porous. When painting directly onto an unprepared concrete wall, much of the first layer of paint will be sucked up by the concrete. Unless the wall has been painted beforehand with at least two coats of quality paint, a huge amount of paint will need to be applied to get the right image quality. It is best to have a qualified painter prepare the wall well before the muralist is ready to commence work. To ensure it is prepared properly, always provide instructions to the contractor – ask for quality paint to be used (as instructed by the artist) and ensure they will do two coats. It's best to include these terms in the subcontractor's contract. Speak to them again before they commence the job to ensure that all is clear, then once the wall has been prepared, carry out a site inspection prior to the installation day to check its condition.

There is No Decision-Maker Onsite

Issue: Your art consultant or art project manager is ready to install the large project you have commissioned. There are numerous factors to take into account, but the main decision-maker on the project (you or perhaps a member of the art committee) is not onsite to answer questions.

Solution: In the early days of Art Pharmacy, we did a project with a heritage building in Melbourne's CBD. We had been working on the project for months. On the day, we had to turn off the tram lines to install the artwork; we had a team of installers, people managing traffic, a boom lift to operate and a heavy artwork to install on the front of the building. However, there was no one there to sign off on the final placement of the artwork. We went ahead, but post-project, we were told the placement was not right.

Always ensure that there is at least one decision-maker present on the day of installation. At Art Pharmacy, we make this a mandatory condition for any job we do. Challenges will often arise which need to be resolved quickly by someone onsite with the power to do so – and they need to be there to resolve them!

Installation is Unsatisfactory	**Issue:** You, your art manager or your committee are unhappy with the placement of the artwork or the final look of installation.

Solution: As with the previous issue, the answer here is to be onsite during the installation. If that is not possible, clearly outline your expected outcome for the install in an email to the team beforehand. Include written details and photos. Make sure you and/or anyone else involved in the project approve and sign off on the installation plan beforehand.

Unwanted Feedback from the Public	**Issue:** Members of the public approach the installers or artist working onsite with unwanted feedback or complaints.

Solution: Section-off the installation area with traffic cones and a sign that details the permission for the artist to work on the site. Include an email address on the sign where people can send their comments or queries.

Traffic Management	**Issue:** There is traffic around and/or near the site that will need to be controlled during installation.

Solution: Traffic control for a public art installation can be expensive and time-consuming. Always be clear who is responsible for traffic control and make sure it is stated in all fee proposals and contracts. Organise, or talk with whoever will organise, any traffic control measures that need to be put into place long in advance of installation day so that you know what to expect – the last thing you want is to be held up by traffic on the day.

Delivery of Artwork

Issue: The courier delivering the artwork or artworks arrives too early, too late or gets lost.

Solution: Ensure you have your courier's mobile number and they have yours. Get to the site early and ask your courier to text you when they are on their way. If you can't be onsite, always have a reliable proxy to do the same. There must be someone there to receive the artwork and to do a condition report. Also, always triple check all loading dock access areas before the installation date and when you arrive onsite so that the courier will be able to deliver the artwork.

Site Access

Issue: On the day of installation, you are unable to access the site.

Solution: Make sure you are onsite early and there is a contact onsite you can speak to. Have all security phone numbers handy, reconfirm access details the day before, fill out and double check any access forms. Talk to security about the installation at least three days before the day and remind them of the timeframe for the install.

Damaged Artworks

Issue: Artwork is delivered damaged or not at the expected standard.

Solution: When the artwork has been completed, always request photos from the artist so you have a reference for what to expect on installation day. If the artist is arranging any framing, make sure you get a detailed description of that as well. Always request that the artist be onsite for installation – in almost all cases, they will want to be there anyway to ensure their artwork is safely delivered.

All artworks should be delivered by a specialist art courier that has the right insurance, or sent through registered, insured post. This will minimise risk of problems. I also advise including a clause in the artist's contract around your expectations of the standard of the work; who is responsible for any damage that the artwork might sustain before, during and after transit; and the level of insurance of the artwork. Make sure you are both clear on who is responsible for the artwork's insurance.

Project Lags   **Issue:** The project is delayed for
months before implementation.

Solution: There can be delays when working on any large development.
People may move off the project; companies may even be sold. If there
are long lags between stages of implementation, your artist may want
to move on to other projects.

If the project timeframe spans more than six months, it is best to
compensate the artist (and any other consultants working on the job) with
a percentage of the project if the delays within that period are three months
or longer. Also, keep them informed about the timing of any delays as best
you can so they can plan ahead.

Artist is Unable   **Issue:** The artist is unable to use the installation
to Use Installation   equipment, such as a boom lift, on the site.
Equipment

Solution: Artists' skills in using equipment for installation varies. Some
experienced artists will have built up their skills over time, but most need
assistance and support for the installation. They may also need support
in adhering to your Safe Work Method Statement (SWMS).

Some larger jobs may involve the use of a boom lift (or similar) to access
hard-to-reach places. If the artist is unable to use this, you may need
to ensure that they have an assistant who can help them. This should
be included in the artist's brief and in their contract.

Be clear on what is expected of the artist and provide them with as much
information on the site and installation processes as you can. If possible,
have them do a site inspection so they can see the area they will be working
in or, at the very least, send photographs of the completed site to them.
Always send this information through at least two weeks before installation.

There will be paperwork that the artist will need to complete around
health and safety before installation day. Ensure all WHS documents are
sent to the artist (or the art consultant for them to pass on to the artist)
four to six weeks before installation and give them a date when they'll
need to get documents back to you.

The artist will also need to provide you with a certificate that shows
what public liability insurance they have. Let them know when they should
submit this to you – preferably early in the project. Most artists understand
that public liability insurance is a must for the site, but if they don't have
insurance, direct them to NAVA or a similar art association that may offer
them a more affordable solution.

Always check what certificates the artist has in advance and/or ask them to gain the necessary qualifications for using equipment if needed. You may wish to work with an external production manager to assist with this.

If working with a heritage site, use the site's own specialist teams when organising and implementing installation.

The Artwork is Unfinished and/or the Worksite is Left Unclean

Issue: The artwork is installed but is left unfinished, or not as expected. The site has not been cleaned after installation.

Solution: Have a decision-maker onsite to review the artwork. If this is not possible, visit the site immediately after installation. Doing this gives you the opportunity to take notes and photograph the artwork and the worksite. If there are issues, call the artist, or the art consultant if you are using one, as soon as possible to discuss. Send a follow-up email immediately with photographs, a written explanation of the issue and notes on how you would like the issue to be resolved. Usually, the artist will return to clean up the site and finish the artwork until you are happy with the outcome.

While it is rare to have problems like this, if they do arise, they should be easy to resolve because there will be an outline of the artist's responsibilities included in their contract, along with the agreed design concept, artist's brief and breakdown of fee payments. The contract will clearly state that a percentage of their fee will be held back until the final artwork and its installation have been approved. Reminding them of this will be a great motivation for them to fix up any issues.

As an example, I once had an artist who installed a printed vinyl artwork onsite even though in their contract it was agreed they would be painting a mural with acrylic and spray paints. The artist decided at some point in the project to illustrate the work on a computer and print the file on vinyl instead. This was not what was agreed, so they had to remove the vinyl from the site and recreate the mural by hand as specified in the artist's brief and their contract.

Artists will sometimes take artistic licence, so it is essential that you clearly outline what you expect from the artwork in their contract.

ART IS
AN
UNDER
ESTIM
ATED
FORCE

THE CREATION OF A LEGACY

Art is an underestimated force in terms of our economy.

MARKETING AND AUDIENCE ENGAGEMENT

Creating an artwork for a public space isn't just about putting an artwork somewhere people can see it – it's about engaging your community with the artwork for years to come.

That is where the idea of the 'fat tail' strategy comes in. I discussed this in detail in my first book, *Making Art Matter*. Think of this fat tail as the tail of a crocodile. Their tail is as much a part of their body as any other part – it's not there for decoration. Without it, a crocodile is not going anywhere! A crocodile's tail is powerful and effective and keeps moving and engaging. So, like a crocodile's tail, the activation of an artwork should be strong and engaging over time, and be reactivated again and again. Also, once the artwork has been installed, you will want to maximise the investment you have made on your project.

Marketing is an essential aspect of keeping that tail moving.

Think about how to market your artwork and the space it is in, and how to draw people to both.

It's important that any artwork in a public place be constantly activated and maintained throughout the years. For example, seasonal marketing ideas that centre around the artwork, such as a Christmas or Lunar New Year event, could draw the community to the artwork year after year.

Start Early

You should start thinking about the marketing of the artwork in the early to mid-stage of the project. On a large project, that would be at least two to three months before the expected installation of the work. We suggest reaching out to your dedicated in-house marketing team early because that way, you and your marketing team will have the energy to do the job well, and have enough time to target and implement the right message you want to communicate.

This message should be relayed through both internal and external communication channels. You want everyone in your organisation, along with stakeholders, to be on the same page about how the artwork will be marketed and publicised well before it is installed onsite. If you have a content or communications team you can work with, get them developing a plan for promotion as early as possible.

How they frame your message will depend on the purpose of your project and what audiences you need to engage with to make it a success. If marketing will be important to the project, you may consider including a member of your media or communications team on your art committee – particularly if they need to be filled in on the project at regular intervals.

If you don't have an in-house marketing team, find an external team to take the work on, or talk to your art consultant and the artist about ways you could market and launch the artwork.

By starting early with your marketing and media plan, you'll have plenty of time to promote related PR and community engagement activities within the local community. Promoting and talking about the art project before the artwork is installed can be done through social media and local forums. For example, your artist may have a great following on social media – your marketing team could liaise with them to tap into this valuable marketing resource. This works both ways and will provide good support to the artist you work with, thereby creating brand equity between them and your organisation.

Similarly, your art consultant will have their own opportunities and outlets for publicising your art project so don't forget to include them in your marketing plan.

One important thing to remember here is to make your intentions around the marketing and publicity of the artwork very clear to the artist early on so that they and the art consultant know what to expect and, more importantly, what is expected of them. You really don't want any miscommunication here, so ensure that these expectations are discussed, confirmed and written into the artist's contract.

Some questions around marketing that should be answered in the artist's contract include:
- Does the artist need to supply a headshot and bio for any marketing material, social media or the artwork launch?
- Will the making of the artwork and installation be documented through video and/or photography? If so, at what stage or stages?
- Will any of the photographs or videos be made available to the artist? (I recommend the inclusion of this in the contract be standard practice.)
- Is the artist expected to attend a launch night? Are they expected to speak?
- Do they need to be available for media enquiries?
- Will the artist be available to do community events such as artist talks or precinct tours? If so, how often and how many?
- How will the artist be reimbursed for events they participate in?

Events and the Cultural Calendar

When planning an event to promote the artwork or, even better, when launching it, consider what other cultural events happen throughout the year. You might find your promotion could tie in with a relevant community event – for example, Lunar New Year, Mardi Gras, NAIDOC Week, National Sustainability Week, etc. Contact your local council and speak to their events and/or arts teams. Find out what is going on in the area and when, and how you can work in with these events. If you and the council can collaborate on an event, or piggyback on an existing one, it will be a win-win situation for both parties.

Artwork Launch and Artist Talks

When your project is complete and the artwork is installed and ready for viewing, a great way to promote it is by hosting a launch.

This gives you and your organisation the opportunity to celebrate the artist and their achievement, and to introduce the local community to the artwork. Invite everyone concerned – the community, stakeholders, people who support the artist, and others in the wider creative community. Make a big deal over it and celebrate. If travel restrictions don't allow for this, then consider holding a virtual launch via Zoom.

I also suggest you ask the artist to do an artist talk for the local community. Getting them talking about their artwork is a wonderful way to share the intention behind the work with your intended audience. This sort of event should be carefully planned by your marketing team with your art consultant and the artist, and timed to coincide with the launch. You may also consider having more than one talk if the artist is willing; perhaps one around the launch and one later, when the community has become more familiar with the artwork. This can work in with your fat tail strategy.

I've included an example event invitation (albeit fictional) here for your reference. Invitations like this, along with pictures of the artwork and the artist as well as any other relevant details, can be promoted on your organisation's website and social media, and displayed on local community noticeboards.

THE CREATION OF A LEGACY

Dear Art Lover,

Join art consultant Emilya Colliver for a glass of wine and a lively conversation with leading mid-career Melbourne-based artist Scarlett Rose to explore the ideas behind her work and practice.

Rose creates unusual, fictional creatures inspired by her own experiences with fauna, and explores how humans perceive the other.

Rose uses decorative materials more usually associated with craft and fashion to create her artworks, questioning the so-called 'uncrossable' line between design and high art.

There will be opportunities for you to ask questions and get involved in the discussion.

Date: Tuesday 15 April 2025	Time: 6pm to 7pm
Event Type: In person at Level 5, 101 Collins Street, Melbourne, 3000	Cost: Free

Note that in these invitations, it is always good to include mention of catering and drinks as this will add extra encouragement for people to turn up.

With events such as these, you can build an understanding and awareness of the fat tail strategy required to make the best of a creative project both in the early groundwork stage and throughout the project's development.

As with all other marketing events, always discuss the idea of a launch or artist talk with the artist well in advance and agree on what is expected of them with such an event. If they are required to contribute to or be a part of any promotion, this should be explained to them early on, included in the artist brief and incorporated into their contract.

Cultural Tourism

I'd like to touch here on cultural tourism and why it is important for your art project and its longevity. There is an exciting injection of interest in Australia's cultural tourism sector because of the runaway successes of art events such as Vivid Sydney in NSW and art sites such as David Walsh's MONA (the Museum of Old and New Art) in Hobart, Tasmania. There is a significant opportunity to weigh up here for developers when planning permanent public artworks or even seasonal temporary projects. While this is not a standard consideration for most corporate art projects, if you are able to make an art statement that draws a national and possibly international crowd, then you will set yourself apart from your competitors. If this is something that interests you, then think about how you can weave this into your project. Art is a significant part of the tourism sector, and it is growing; perhaps this growth can benefit your project, too.

Consider how your art project could help create, contribute to or reinvigorate your site. Could your art project inspire tourist spend in the area?

Could it become another reason to visit the area, another reason to stick around longer, another reason for people to mention it to their friends when asked for tips on interesting places to go or see? Could it be something to take a photograph of and share with others? Is it Instagrammable?

Retail developers and asset managers already benefit from this consideration, inviting more dollars into their assets, but councils and state governments can also harness this to stimulate people to visit and diversify tourism spend across the state. This can only work to the benefit of local businesses and the robustness of the economy and sector. A great example of this is what MONA has done for Tasmania's tourism economy.

Many retail and property corporations are including tourism experts in their teams. This is a growing and productive trend and is worth considering when planning your art project.

Documentation

Once your artwork is complete, it will require documentation – photographs of the artwork will need to be taken, an artwork plaque designed and information put together to ensure the ongoing maintenance of the piece. Some of this information can also be used by your marketing department for promotional purposes.

As with other elements of the marketing of your project, if you want the artist to be involved in any documentation of the artwork, let them know in advance and put it in their contract so it is clear what expectations you have of them around this.

Photography and Video

I highly recommend engaging a professional photographer and videographer to document the artwork at various times throughout the project, depending on what the artist has agreed to. These professionals can photograph and film the artist in action and document the artwork's progress at the artist's studio, at the fabricator's studio, and during and after installation onsite. They can document the launch of the artwork and any other promotional events, including artist talks.

These key content types are essential for marketing and should be planned and budgeted for early on. For example, a video of the artist talking about the project and what it means is a fantastic way to promote the project. Photographs and video help create brand power and advocate your support for the broader creative community.

Visuals can also be used to communicate to others within your organisation where you are up to in the project. Images of the artwork are very useful to share with stakeholders at committee meetings and can create a buzz about the project.

If you do wish to document the art-making process, ensure that the artist is aware of what you intend and have this written into their contract. I suggest you share these photographs and videos with the artist so they can use them to promote their practice.

I recommend writing a photography or videography brief outlining what you want, and be clear about your expectations. As with the brief for your artist, this outline should ensure that the creative practitioner you employ will provide you with the best outcome. For example, in addition to images of the final artwork, if you need a headshot of the artist or intend the process to be documented throughout, then specify these in the photography brief.

I will go into further detail about documentation later in this chapter.

Brochure and Press Release

The marketing team can use the professional photographs you commission for a variety of materials, including a brochure about the artist and a press release about the project. If they do this, then you may wish to enlist a copywriter to help craft an artist bio. They could also write up a case study that you can put into your organisation's portfolio and share with the artist.

Plaques

It is important that the artist is acknowledged with a plaque that credits them as the creator of the artwork. This should be placed as close to the artwork as is practical. The plaque's text should include the artist's full name, the title of the artwork, the year of creation and a short artist statement about the work. Proper attribution of the artwork to the artist is part of their moral right to the artwork.

The following is an example of the text for an artwork plaque installed in the public realm. Art Pharmacy made it for an artwork included in a 2021 project we did with Place Management NSW and The Rocks. For the plaque, we used a high-resolution full-colour dye-sublimation print for the text on a white gloss aluminium art panel suitable for the outdoor environment.

Maddison Gibbs
Spirits Make Noise, 2021
'My work is about the regeneration of Country, culture and women.'

Maddison Gibbs is a proud Barkindji woman who grew up in Dubbo, NSW. She currently lives and works between Sydney and Kandos, NSW. Both artist and activist, Gibbs' practice examines dual histories, focusing on past and present Aboriginal cultural narratives. A multidisciplinary artist, Gibbs works across a wide spectrum of cultural practice; her current focus is the telling of women's stories.

The dual sensitivities of caring for Country and fighting injustice is an interesting tension that Gibbs explores. This work is inspired by Aboriginal female ancestors and the resurgence of the female matriarch who fights for Country and community. The artwork imagery is drawn from seeds, nuts, plants and medicine. The spirits represented in these drawings reflect the many roles that women hold: grandma, aunty, sister, daughter, niece, mother, life-giver and baby. Women have been the backbone of ancient and contemporary culture since the beginning of time; this work explores ancient Aboriginal cultural practices that are embedded in the sustainable and ongoing care of our Country and in our communities. It is a call and response to individual accountability and action.

Explore more about the artist and artwork by scanning the QR code below. Commissioned by Place Management NSW, The Rocks and Art Pharmacy.

Note the use of a QR code here – always a good idea for a public artwork. The logos of the commissioning bodies were included on the plaque as well.

Other Acknowledgements
Always credit the art consultant or art curator who has helped you deliver your project. Some organisations forget to do this. Crediting them shows you support the consultant's practice – after all, an art consultant's brand has creative cultural capital.

GOLDEN POINTS

01 Make the most of the time and money
you spend on your art project by investing
in a fat tail strategy of marketing
and community engagement.

02 Think about cultural tourism and
how it can be part of your art project.

03 Use photography and video to
document and promote the project.

04 Always credit the artist for their
artwork with a plaque. Remember
to credit your art consultant, too!

The Photography Brief

As with the artist, the professional photographer and videographer you hire will need guidance in the form of a detailed brief so that they have clarity around your expectations. This is important as you will be using their images to document the artwork; to market it before, during and after the launch; and to promote the artwork well into the future to support your fat tail strategy. So, feel free to employ art dating principles in this scenario as well! Always look at any potential candidate's portfolio of previous work so you can get a feel for their style and see if it will suit your needs.

In this chapter, I'll outline how to write a brief for your photographer. Note that the brief for a videographer would be a little different, but similar. To start with, include some basics:

- name of the project
- aim of the project – provide a short summary of the 'why'
- full address and contact details for access to the artwork
- dates when you would like them to take the photos.
  This is especially important if you expect them to cover
  specific events, such as the artwork launch
- their fee, which will vary depending on whether they will do half-day
  or full-day shoots
- the outline of a wet weather contingency plan if the artwork is outside
- date for the delivery or transfer of the images.

In addition, give the photographer some guidance on what you do and don't want. Here are some general rules I like to include in the brief:

- Use good lighting. Avoid dark or overexposed images and ensure
  there are no shadows across the artwork.
- Include varied and interesting framing of the images that offer
  different perspectives of the artwork (for example, specify
  landscape or portrait, or if you want them to include a person
  in the foreground to give the photograph some context).
- Ensure the images are beautiful, sharp and striking – they need
  to be visually arresting.
- Include close-up and far shots.
- Ensure the artwork or subject is in focus and blur
  the background/foreground.
- Avoid taking pictures of people with phones or masks.
- Avoid taking pictures of people frowning, blinking or squinting.

Style of Photograph

It's good to have a familiarity with different types of artwork shots so you can specify what you want in the photography brief. The following are all excellent ways to photograph an artwork. Let the photographer know what kind of shots you like – show them examples if you have some so that they have a good chance of capturing what you want.

Artwork Image: In this type of image, the artwork is centred in the frame and shown in its entirety. It is also useful if the photographer can take this in a way that shows the size of the artwork.

Artwork Close-up: A close-up shot of the artwork, either as a cropped image or taken by zooming in, is great for showing intricate details.

The Artwork in Situ: It's always good to show the context of the artwork by showing part or all of the space where the artwork is located.

The Artwork with the Artist: A great image for marketing is one that includes the artist, or one that shows the artist creating or installing the artwork.

The Artwork and the General Public: Images of the general public interacting with the artwork are also fantastic for publicity.

Number of Images

Ideally, the photographer should provide at least four to six usable images of the artwork. So that would be at least one artwork image, one close-up or detail, one artwork in situ and one with some sort of interaction of people with the artwork. These would be taken after the artwork has been installed, but you may also want your photographer to take photos of the artwork's progress during the project. This might include images taken at the artist's studio (if this has been negotiated with the artist) and later, during installation. If this is the case, you should include details of this in the photography brief.

Always specify the resolution and file format you require. At Art Pharmacy, we request high-resolution images (1600 px wide) as well as low-resolution versions (under 400 kB) in landscape format for use on our website. Don't forget to ask the photographer to provide you with at least one image in portrait format suitable for social media such as Instagram.

One important thing to remember when using the photographer's images in your marketing is you must always credit them – they are artists in their own right. This is best practice.

Naming Images

Each photo file should be clearly labelled by the photographer with your name, the name of the artwork or artist, and their name and date. For example: ArtPharmacy_ScarlettRose_MaterialDisco_03_03_25.jpg

Delivery

Make sure you specify how you would like the photographs delivered
to you. For example, you could say in your brief:

Please share all files within folders labelled 'High Res for print',
'Low Res for web' and 'Social Media' in a Dropbox folder or shared drive.
Be very specific as to what sharing platform your organisation uses
so that the photographer is clear on where they will need to put the files.

Timeframe

As outlined earlier in the chapter, always specify when you want
the images. For example, you could say in your brief that you'll want
the images no later than five days after the photography shoot.

The Photographer's Contract

Just as you have a contract with the artist, you will need to create an
appropriate contract for the photographer that clearly outlines your
expectations and their responsibilities regarding the work. Include all
the information they will need to know to carry out the job, as well as
details of their fee and the expected dates of delivery. Doing this will
ensure you are both on the same page and will minimise the chances
of misinterpretation by either party of the job's requirements.

GOLDEN POINTS

01 Professional images will form an integral part of your marketing and will be a useful tool to support your fat tail strategy.

02 When considering hiring a photographer or videographer, make sure you review their portfolio to see what kind of work they do.

03 Always provide your photographer and videographer with a clear brief and contract. Be clear about what you expect and when.

04 Always credit your photographer, because they are also artists in their own right.

 THE CREATION OF A LEGACY

THE LIFETIME OF THE ARTWORK

When you embark on an art project, think about the lifetime of the artwork. You should have a clear idea of how long you expect the artwork to be in its position, so identify whether it is a temporary, short-term or permanent piece. The life expectancy of the artwork feeds into the brief and the agreement with the artist.

Lifetime of the Artwork and the Maintenance Report

It is best to document your expectations around the life of the artwork in a maintenance report that covers all the information required to maintain its upkeep. After all, **an artwork is an investment and it will need to be looked after!**

Some questions to consider here include:
- How long will the artwork be in its allocated position on the site?
- If it is a permanent or long-term artwork, what will the yearly budget be for its maintenance?
- If it is a temporary artwork, when will it be removed or dismantled?
- If it will be removed at some stage, will your organisation or the artist repurpose the work?
- If it is to be dismantled, will your organisation or the artist handle this? (Note that some artists do repurpose their artworks. This is also a sustainable way of handing the artwork.)
- Will the artwork need to be moved over the course of its lifetime?
- If the artwork needs to be moved, who will be responsible for moving it? Are there specialists that will need to do this? (If so, include their details.)
- If the artwork is to be moved by your organisation, do you have clear instructions from the artist on how to move the artwork?
- If it is to be moved, do you have a place to move it to? For example, elsewhere on the same site, to a different site owned by your organisation or to a new owner's site? Or will it be returned to the artist?
- Do you have care instructions for the maintenance of the artwork, including cleaning? For example, what should it be cleaned with? What cleaning agents should be avoided? How often should it be cleaned?
- If it is a mural, do you have specific cleaning instructions or the details of specialist cleaners that could be contacted if it becomes graffitied?
- If it is a digital artwork, when will the license end and what digital content will replace it at that time, if any?

Comprehensive answers to these questions, along with the artist's and art consultant's details, must be included in your maintenance report. That way, it can serve as a clear and concise handover document for those who will care for the artwork, now and in the future.

Moving the Artwork

The artist will likely want to stay involved with the artwork once it is installed on the site. If at some stage you need to move the artwork, then it is best practice to contact the artist in advance, even if it is just to notify them. This shows that you acknowledge the artist as the creator of the artwork, that it remains their intellectual property and that you wish to preserve the integrity of their artwork. Consulting and involving the artist in the artwork's relocation shows you respect the artist and their work.

Often, the artist will want to have the opportunity to be involved in the artwork's relocation, removal or deinstallation. They might also want to be involved in its maintenance and any repairs it may require. It's important that the artist has a say in what happens to their work when the art project is complete, so include an outline of this in their contract, especially if they want their involvement to be an ongoing commitment. The contract should detail what is expected of each party over the lifetime of the artwork.

With permanent pieces, artists will often have a clear idea about what they want to happen if the artwork needs to be removed from the site. They might request to have the first right of refusal to take it back. They might suggest that it be offered up for sale by their gallery or to a particular client or organisation, so give them an opportunity to submit a proposal for its repositioning or repurposing. Again, these points should be covered in the contract between you and the artist. It's a good idea to be clear about the lifecycle of the artwork from the very beginning.

If it is a temporary installation, the artist may want to deinstall and/or repurpose the artwork, or at least specify how they want it removed and stored. Deinstallation should be factored into the artist's fee, and you should not remove the artwork without the artist's permission.

If you plan to relocate the work, then let your marketing team know. They can then publicise the new location, which will play into your fat tail strategy. Even with a permanent artwork, it's useful for you and your marketing team to regularly revisit and highlight the project so you can engage audiences with the artwork again and again.

Maintenance Manual

The responsibility for sites can change over time, as can their uses. For example, the management of a site might be transferred from one government department to another. Ownership can change, too – your organisation, who originated the project, might decide to sell the site. These things can sometimes make it tricky to manage the artwork over the long term. Artworks might get overlooked, or if the originating team leaves, the new organisation may be left without information about the artwork. This is where a detailed maintenance report and clear documentation of the project (perhaps in a case study) can be useful – so consider what you can do early on, even in the planning stage, to implement this. It's another reason to fully document the project from the concept stage through to completion and beyond. Passing on this documentation to the next managers or owners of the site helps to ensure the artwork will be taken care of. Remember to store this documentation in a way that people can access it in the future. For example, a website of the project is an ideal way to easily share information.

The artwork should also be registered with the local council and this information added to your documentation. Unfortunately, at time of writing, there is no national register for public artworks in Australia. The only alternatives are to register with your local council, create a Wikipedia page for the artwork or have the existence of your work recorded on a relevant site, such as www.monumentaustralia.org.au.

To help you with this documentation process, ensure that the artist supplies you with a clear and detailed maintenance manual once they complete the artwork. This should outline the information for the artwork's plaque, including the artwork's name, year of creation, materials used and an artist statement. (Note that QR codes are sometimes used on artwork plaques and these will need to be kept up to date. Ensure this task is documented in the maintenance manual as well.)

The manual provided by the artist should not only clearly outline the general maintenance required, but also how often the maintenance should be carried out. For example, what should the artwork be cleaned with and how often should it be cleaned?

Along with a list of the materials used, the artist should detail the suppliers they purchased them from and the warranties on each (where applicable) so that if any part of the artwork is damaged or needs replacing, you'll know what to do. Similarly, if paint has been used in a large area of the artwork, ask the artist to include colour swatches in case the artwork needs to be retouched. If the artist decides they want to be involved in any repairs the artwork may require, establish this early on and contact them if the artwork sustains any damage. Having a clear maintenance manual will help to lengthen the life of the artwork and ensure it always looks its best.

GOLDEN POINTS

01 With public art, always think long term. When you move onto another project, what legacy will you leave? Ensure you leave clear documentation that can be passed on to the artwork's next caretaker.

02 Think about the lifetime of the artwork. If you decide to move it from the site, can it be moved to another location where the public can see it? This could then be part of your fat tail strategy.

03 The artist may want to be involved in the maintenance, repair, deinstallation, removal, relocation or dismantling of the artwork if required.

04 Ensure the artist provides you with a detailed maintenance manual.

THE IMPACT OF ART

There are many ways that art can make an impact in our society, in our community and in business. It can support the economy, create social change, bring people together and still be something that we enjoy on a daily basis.

Return on Investment

Art is an underestimated force in terms of our economy.

I believe it can have a significant impact – not so much from the direct expenditure on the artwork itself, but from the increased revenue generated by more visitors coming to an area with art in it, better productivity from those who experience art in the workplace and the free publicity (such as Instagram posts) that public art creates.

'Return on investment' (ROI) is a financial metric that is widely used to measure a project's success. You might consider assessing your ROI on your art project by tracking the economic activity around the site, such as the expenditure in local cafés since the art has been installed or gauging how many more people visit the area.

A good example of a successful ROI on an art project is MONA. Two months after David Walsh opened MONA, ABC News reported that Hotels.com saw a spike in its Hobart bookings of 40%.[21]

In another example of the impact of art on economy, *The Guardian* reports:

Big data analytics of flickr and other social media photo sites in the UK found that neighbourhoods which have a higher proportion of 'art' photographs also have greater relative gains in property prices. Since the development of the art-based Millennium Park in Chicago, violent crime in the area has reduced 27%.[22]

These examples are impressive and obviously great for business, but the real value of art is so much more than this – I believe it is immeasurable. Great art can impact positively on our health and can change how we think and feel. Aside from looking at the economic impact of public art on a business district, consider the many passers-by taking selfies with the artwork, admiring it and enjoying being around the art.

<hr>

21   ABC News, Capital gains: How MONA got Hobart humming,
2016, www.abc.net.au/news/2016-01-13/mona-got-hobart-humming/7081376?
nw=0&r=HtmlFragment
22   The Guardian, Public art: the feel good hit that
makes us linger and spend money, 2017 www.pressreader.com/australia/
the-guardian-australia/20170621/281792809024344

We can think more creatively around how we assess the value of art; at the same time as tracking its economic impact, we should track the difference it can make to a community's wellbeing – after all, they are the audience for the work.

Wellbeing in the Workplace

It is not only in the public arena that art can have an impact on wellbeing. Having good art in our workplaces can have a positive impact on staff, too. Keeping staff happy and morale high in a large organisation isn't easy. According to QuikShift:

A large survey published by the Australian Industry Group (AIG) in 2015 estimated that absenteeism directly costs organisations $578 per employee per day of absence. In direct costs alone, the loss to the economy is said to be in excess of $44 billion per annum.[23] This is an astonishing amount. Now, since COVID-19, getting people back into the office after months of working from home can be even harder. However, I believe art can help to make a difference.

Staff Engagement Ideas

Following are a few ways to use creativity and art to support the wellbeing of your staff. They are also great for encouraging staff engagement with art.

01 **Place a focus on mental health.** This can be done through creative art workshops, art therapy groups or taking a local art tour (of street art, for example). For the art tours, you could employ someone external to do this or think about asking a different staff member each month to tailor a tour. Give them some parameters – perhaps limit the tour to three hours with four stops on the way. Provide a budget and a time limit for research. Walking and seeing something new are wonderful forms of therapy and can help to focus the mind and spirit.

---

23   www.aigroup.com.au/resourcecentre/resource-centre-blogs/hr-blogs/is-it-time-you-attended-to-absenteeism-in-your-business/

02   **Grow your staff's knowledge.** You might start with Friday afternoon drinks and bring in an external expert who can talk with your team about art. This will help develop the art confidence of your people and give them a chance to learn about what art they enjoy. You could also ask your team who they would like to see speak. Alternatively, think about starting a staff art club, encourage different kinds of events and catering (such as a tea or wine tasting and painting evening), or organise visits to art galleries.

03   **Expand your community.** If you are part of a large organisation, connect with (or develop) a mission-driven network in your office. See how art can be involved or make a statement around this. If you have a small business, perhaps join up to local social-impact drives. Learn from your local area. Get involved at the grassroots level.

04   **Nurture your people's passions.** Be inspired by the valuable contribution your staff make to your community every day and encourage them to pursue their passions. You might have many creative pioneers in your organisation that you could encourage – you just have to identify them!

05   **Host art exhibitions in the foyer of your office building.** This can get your staff engaged in art and make an impact on visitors to the building. This is a great way to build community engagement.

Social Impact

Libraries and parks are now mandated in our society – they're popping up around the country like mushrooms after rain, which is wonderful to see. They support a community's wellbeing and help to bring people together by creating a public space that is important to the whole community. I believe public art can do the same. The mandatory inclusion of public art on new development projects is a step in the right direction. However, there is still more work to do.

As Stuart Cunningham explored in his paper, 'You're hot,
then you're cold: Creative industries policy making in Australia'[24]:

*Much compelling evidence has emerged over the last two decades
demonstrating the importance of Australia's creative industries. In 2014,
the Australian Bureau of Statistics confirmed that culture is 'big business'
in this country. Yet despite this, interest by policy makers at all levels
of government has been intermittent, at best.*

The creation of appropriate policies for the arts in Australia has been left
as an 'unfinished agenda'. Until the time this issue is addressed, I'd like to
see internal policies around art set by private companies and corporations.
Doing this will make it easier to make decisions around art and creative
projects, and reduce the amount of red tape these projects tend to involve.
If this is done at senior level, I can see a move like this encouraging creative
pioneers and art implementers. I do feel that for-profit organisations
should make a pact to support art and culture; it shouldn't be left to the
government or councils to push the agenda of supporting creatives. I'd like
organisations to look at supporting the arts not as a risk but as a positive
initiative that can enhance the workplace and its culture. These initiatives
will not only benefit the organisation, but encourage and support the next
generation of creatives and artists.

I have encountered large developers that expect great things on a small
budget. They believe that art is not worth investing in for their project or their
staff's wellbeing and because of this, they fail to support our consultancy
and the artists we work with. They may want artwork their marketing team
can shout about, but they do not respect the arts.

I hope to see a growing number of senior managers developing
healthy partnerships and collaborations with art consultancies, artists
and small arts organisations. I know they can learn about what their staff
are interested in supporting; it's as easy as doing a staff survey to get
constructive feedback. For any organisation, building a relationship with art
shouldn't stem from the marketing team wanting to make the organisation
look good; it should be incorporated deep into the company's soul.

In post-pandemic times, many employees are looking for reasons
to stay with organisations that commit to something they're passionate
about, otherwise they will simply move on. Art can be that thing for your
organisation. There is a big movement in business around increasing social
capital and the wellbeing of employees that is making large organisations
rethink the way they do things. My suggestion here is to work directly with
your staff to see what they're doing and what causes they support or would
consider supporting. There is so much to learn in this space.

---

24   Cunningham, Stuart, 2015, 'You're hot, then you're cold:
Creative industries policy making in Australia', eprints.qut.edu.au/89368/

Art Pharmacy's Commitment

Globally, there are new ideas sprouting up around art and its role in our community. There has been a move for artists to address social issues and the rise of various cultural movements with their art, and there is an increased initiative for art to create a social impact.

With this in mind, Art Pharmacy applied for B Corporation certification in 2020. A business can be awarded a B Corporation certificate by:

meeting high standards of verified performance, accountability, and transparency on factors from employee benefits and charitable giving to supply chain practices and input materials.[25]

I am proud to say that in mid-2022, Art Pharmacy was awarded B Corp certification. We are committed to the values of all B Corps – we seek to build trust with our clients, suppliers, community and employees. We hope to attract like-minded collaborators and investors. We strongly believe that for-profit companies can support networks and supply chains, pay for them fairly and deal with them honestly and with the highest regard.

We sought to gain this status as we support this movement and believe it can benefit the creative community. We also wanted to show all the people we work with our commitment to what we do. I've included this information here to provide you with a bit of food for thought. If we are committed to social change, perhaps your organisation could be, too. Could you be the next organisation to apply for B Corp certification?

The Future

I believe a greater focus on the arts, artists and creatives in our community (in Australia and globally) will encourage creativity and lead to innovation. This, in turn, will result in art projects that support the community's wellbeing, make both a social and economic impact and instigate change.

So, now is the time to be brave. Set policies around art in your business. Start an art project. Champion the arts by becoming a creative pioneer or support someone you know to become an art implementer
… the possibilities are endless.

And remember: go gently and do it authentically but also dare to step out of your comfort zone!

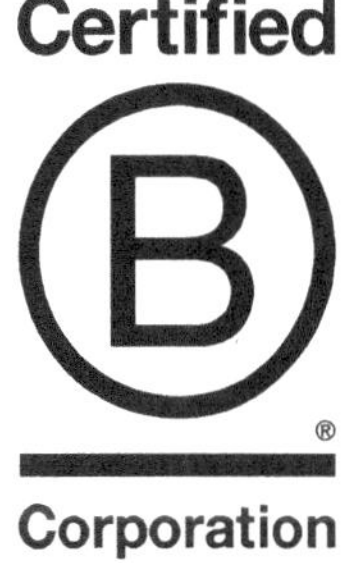

---

25   B Corporation, bcorporation.net/about-b-corps

REFERENCES

ART PHARMACY

In addition to Art Pharmacy, we now have our new digital art branch, Sugar Glider Digital, up and running.

artpharmacy.com.au
www.sugarglider.digital

PLACEMAKING

Bloomberg Associates, 2019, *Asphalt Art Guide: How to Reclaim City Roadways and Public Infrastructure with Art*, Bloomberg Philanthropies, data.bloomberglp.com/dotorg/sites/43/2019/10/asphalt-art-guide.pdf

Hamdi, Nabeel., 2010, *The Placemaker's Guide to Building Community: Earthscan Tools for Community Planning*, Routledge, Oxfordshire, UK.

International WELL Building Institute (IWBI), www.wellcertified.com/about-iwbi

Placemaking Week, placemakingactionweek.com

Project for Public Spaces, www.pps.org

Project for Public Spaces, What is Placemaking?, 2007, www.pps.org/article/what-is-placemaking

State Government of Victoria, Urban Design Guidelines for Victoria, www.planning.vic.gov.au/policy-and-strategy/urban-design/urban-design-guidelines

ACCESSIBILITY

Accessible Arts, NSW, www.aarts.net.au

RESOURCE MANAGEMENT

Artwork Archive, www.artworkarchive.com/public-art

TENDERS

Australian Tenders, info.australiantenders.com.au/blog/what-is-a-tender

Enns, Blair, 2010, *The Win Without Pitching Manifesto*, RockBench Publishing Corp, www.winwithoutpitching.com/the-manifesto

CULTURE AND CREATIVITY

Australian Bureau of Statistics, Australian National Accounts: Cultural and Creative Activity Satellite Accounts, Experimental, 2008-09, 2009, www.abs.gov.au/ausstats/abs@.nsf/latestproducts/5271.0main%20features32008-09

CultureCounts, culturecounts.cc

Florida, Richard, 2003, *The Rise of the Creative Class … and how it's transforming work, leisure, community, & everyday life*, Basic Books.

Arts Law Centre for Australia, 2017, Artists in the Black Collaboration Toolkit – resources for use in Indigenous art projects, www.artslaw.com.au/information-sheet/artists-in-the-black-collaboration-toolkit-resources-for-use-in-indigenous/

Government Architect New South Wales, 2020, Better Placed: Draft Connecting with Country – A draft framework for understanding the value of Aboriginal knowledge in the design and planning of places, www.governmentarchitect.nsw.gov.au/resources/ga/media/files/ga/discussion-papers/draft-connecting-with-country-framework-2020-11-12.pdf

Janke, Terri, 2016, *Indigenous Cultural Protocols and the Arts: A book of case studies,* Terri Janke and Company Pty Ltd, www.terrijanke.com.au/indigenous-cultural-protocols-and-arts

Janke, Terri, 2021, *True Tracks: Respecting Indigenous knowledge and culture,* UNSW Press

ART AND CULTURE POLICY

Cunningham, Stuart, 2013, *Hidden Innovation: Policy, Industry and the Creative Sector,* University of Queensland Press.

Cunningham, Stuart, 2015, You're hot, then you're cold: Creative industries policy making in Australia, In Ashton, P, Colley, L, & Andersen, L (Eds.) *Creative business in Australia: Learnings from the Creative Industries Innovation Centre, 2009 to 2015,* UTS ePRESS, eprints.qut.edu.au/89368

Kabanda, Patrick, 2018, *The Creative Wealth of Nations,* Cambridge University Press.

Throsby, David, 2001, *Economics and Culture,* Cambridge University Press.

Throsby, David, 2010, *The Economics of Cultural Policy,* Cambridge University Press.

LEGAL AND COPYRIGHT

Arts Law, www.artslaw.com.au

Copyright Agency, www.copyright.com.au

National Association for the Visual Arts (NAVA), visualarts.net.au

SUSTAINABILITY

United Nations, 2016, Department of Economic and Social Affairs, Sustainable Development, The 17 Goals, sdgs.un.org/goals

BUSINESS

Art Business Info. for Artists, www.artbusinessinfo.com/copyright-in-australia.html

B Corporation (this initiative began in the USA but is now a global movement), www.bcorporation.net/en-us/ www.bcorporation.com.au/

Burlingham, Bo, 2005, *Small Giants: Companies that Choose to be Great Instead of Big,* Penguin Group USA.

Enns, Blair, 2018, *Pricing Creativity: A guide to profit beyond the billable hour,* www.winwithoutpitching.com/pricing-creativity/

Sinek, Simon, 2009, *Start with Why: How great leaders inspire everyone to take action,* Portfolio, Penguin Group USA.

Sinek, Simon, 2009, *Start with Why: How great leaders inspire action*, TEDx, www.youtube.com/watch?v=u4ZoJKF_VuA

Bakhshi, Hasan, Hargreaves, Ian and Mateos-Garcia, Juan, A Manifesto for the Creative Economy, NESTA, www.nesta.org.uk/report/a-manifesto-for-the-creative-economy

Small Giants Academy (a small Melbourne company inspired by the book *Small Giants* by Bo Burlingham), www.smallgiants.com.au

DIGITAL CONTENT

Australian Government Department of Communications, Information Technology and the Arts, 2006, *Unlocking the potential: Digital Content Industry Action Agenda – Strategic Industry Leaders Group report to the Australian Government, November 2005*, apo.org.au/sites/default/files/resource-files/2006-03/apo-nid2166.pdf

Cunningham, Stuart, Cutler, Terry, Ryan, Mark; Hearn, Greg and Keane, Michael, Research and Innovation Systems in the Production of Digital Content and Applications, Creative Industries Cluster Study, Volume III, 2021.

NFTS

Bowden, James and Thomas Jones, Edward, NFT's are much bigger than an art fad – here's how they could change the world, *The Conversation*, 2021, theconversation.com/nfts-are-much-bigger-than-an-art-fad-heres-how-they-could-change-the-world-159563

Morris, Doosie, 'It's chaos for a lot of people': What is the future of NFT art in Australia?, *The Guardian Australia*, 2021, www.theguardian.com/artanddesign/2021/may/19/its-chaos-for-a-lot-of-people-what-is-the-future-of-nfts-in-australian-art

Shaw, Anny, NFT breakthrough: Ethereum co-founder Joe Lubin creates 99% energy efficient blockchain—and Damien Hirst is its first artist, *The Art Newspaper*, 2021, www.theartnewspaper.com/2021/03/30/nft-breakthrough-ethereum-co founder-joe-lubin-creates-99percent-energy-efficient-blockchainand-damien-hirst-is-its-first-artist

Thompson, Clive, The Untold Story of the NFT Boom, *New York Times Magazine*, 2021, www.nytimes.com/2021/05/12/magazine/nft-art-crypto.html

Wintermeyer, Lawrence, Bitcoin's Energy Consumption is a Highly Charged Debate – Who's Right?, *Forbes*, 2021 www.forbes.com/sites/lawrencewintermeyer/2021/03/10/bitcoins-energy-consumption-is-a-highly-charged-debate--whos-right/?sh=4eeeb0427e78

OTHER

McKeown, Greg, 2014, *Essentialism: The disciplined pursuit of less*, Ebury Publishing (a Random House Group Company).

Plotkin, Bill, 2003, *Soulcraft: Crossing into the mysteries of nature and psyche*, New World Library.

ACKNOWLEDGEMENTS

Together with everyone at Art Pharmacy, I would like to thank all the artists we have had the pleasure of working with on so many projects over the years. Each of you create art from your soul and you are all our inspiration.

Thank you to my dear friends, who keep me grounded when my wheels start to wobble: Mandy Drury, Jaye Alderson, Elise Slater and Georgia Rickard; to Ian Neil SC for making my cheeks hurt with laughter. To my painting friend Peter Tzannes; and to my Melbourne counterpart Sarah, who is a true creative working in a not-for-profit organisation for over 8 years – you never cease to be an inspiration to me.

I would like to acknowledge and thank my team at Art Pharmacy, Brunella, Claire, Zeta and Margaux. To the sisters, Paris and Beau Neilson thank you for your support & friendship over the years.

To my English connection and James Birch and Jane Rankin-Reid.

Thank you to Kathleen for the re-development edit of this book.

Thank you to the Entrepreneurs' Organization (EO) Sydney network, including a special thank you to the women of EO of whom I am particularly fond: Kim, Sophia, Victoria, Tracy and Simone.

Thank you to Dominik and Heidi for offering their whimsical cottage in Blackheath in the Blue Mountains so I could finish the editing of this book by the fire. It was an escape from business and family life for a few brief days.

To Amery for typesetting the whole book and the illustrations – always a pleasure!

Thank you to the School of Shamanic Womancraft and their 4SJ (Four Seasons Journey) program held in the Blue Mountains, postponed so many times over the past 24 months due to COVID-19. I made a promise over a spitting fire (eek yes) to finish this book on a moon eclipse and print it in 2022, and so it has been done!! I offer thanks to my spirit guides, the snow leopard and the sugar glider, the latter of which inspired the name of my new business, Sugar Glider Digital. The sugar glider has taught me to trust the free fall.

Thank you to Giles, my wonderful husband and partner of 20 years, for our time together in Beijing, London and now Sydney.

To my grandmothers and my ancestors, fighters who challenged the norm, fleeing to Australia for a new life, I realise I have your blood pumping in me and take that fighting spirit from you all.

For all those who are creative pioneers challenging the rule book and championing the reasons why art and culture are important, and for those who decide to follow their hearts and their soul, know that the path less travelled is never easy but always exciting and rewarding.

I am truly grateful for all the supporters of Art Pharmacy, and for all my readers for reading right to this last paragraph. Thank you for your support! My last wish here is that you take some of the teachings in this book and use them in your own lives to create impact. We only have one life – live it with passion and creativity.

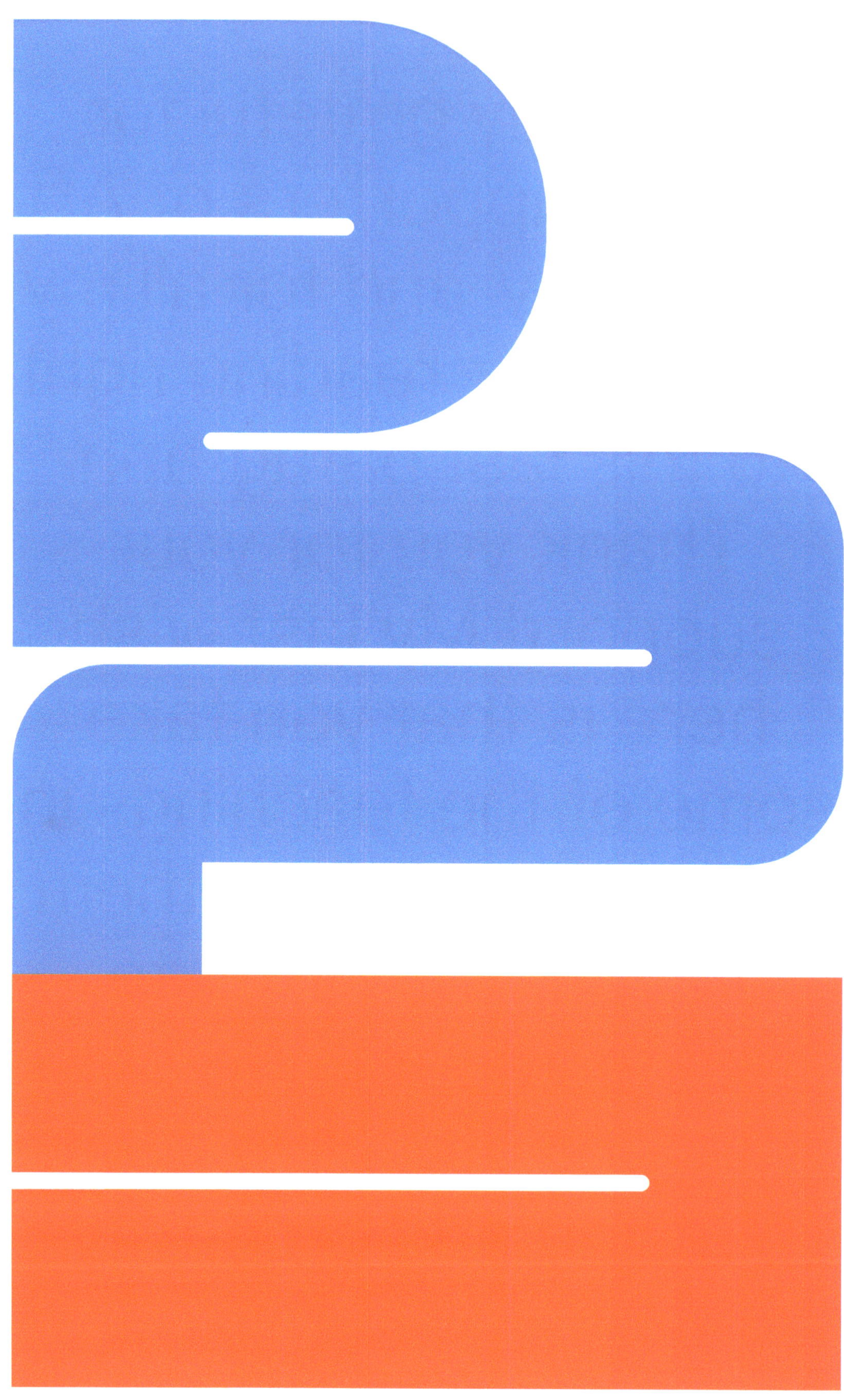

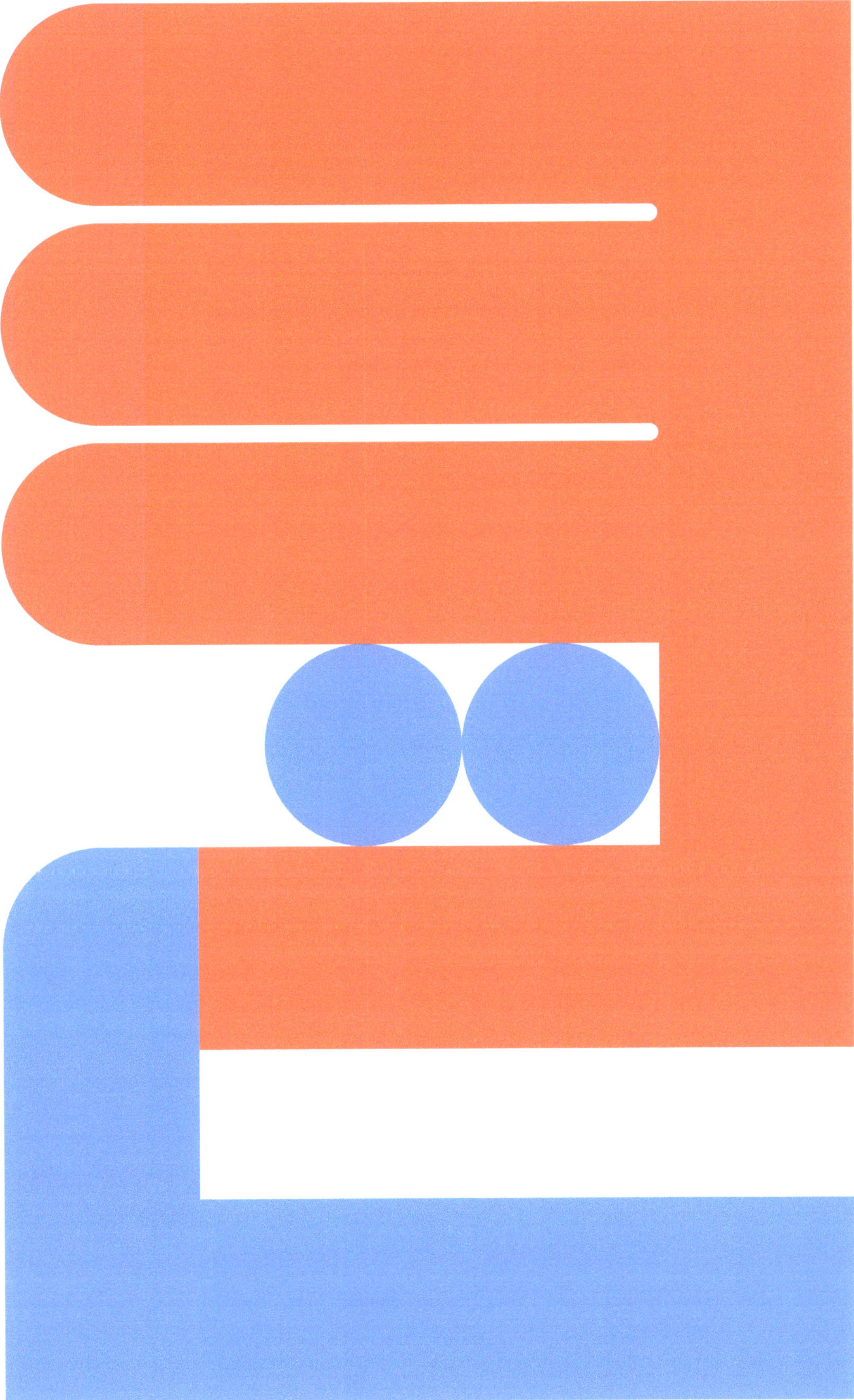